SOCIAL HISTORY OF

TIBET, CHINA

Documented and Illustrated

CHIEF EDITORS

JIN HUI   REN YINONG   MA NAIHUI

DESIGNER

JIZHI   CAI RONG

MANAGING EDITOR

YANG JIMING

图书在版编目 (CIP) 数据

中国西藏社会历史资料：英文／金晖等主编． — 新1版．
北京：五洲传播出版社·1994.11
本书原由中国民族摄影艺术出版社1991年5月出版
ISBN 7-80113-022-7

I.中… II. 金… III. ①地方史—中国—西藏—图集—英文
②西藏封建农奴制—史料—图集—英文 IV.K297.5

中国版本图书馆CIP数据核字 (95) 第 15210 号

中国西藏社会历史资料

五洲传播出版社出版发行

中国北京北三环中路 31 号
邮政编码:100088
1995 年 2 月第一版第一次印刷
787×1092mm 1/16 6 印张
ISBN 7－80113－022－7/Z·18(英)

©1995 by China Intercontinental Press

  31 Beisanhuanzhonglu, Beijing
  100088, China

Sketch Map of the Tibet Autonomous Region

CONTENTS

INTRODUCTION

Tibet, a region of China, is a beautiful, mysterious and enchanting land, located on the "roof of the world." To help friends concerned about Tibet to gain a better understanding, we have written this book on the basis of the "An Exhibition of Materials on the Social History of Tibet, China" sponsored by the Cultural Palace of Nationalities. It illustrates, in brief, the historical relations between Tibet and the central areas of China, and of the Tibetan society under feudal serfdom before 1959. We hope that the book can solve some of the probelms that interest our readers.

PART ONE

TIBET —AN INSEPARABLE PART OF CHINA

From the 7th to the 10th century

In the Tang Dynasty: Close Relations Between Tibet and Central China

The friendly relations between the Tibetan nationality and the Han nationality of the main areas of China can be traced to ancient times, as is proved by archaeological findings and historical documents in Tibetan and Chinese. In the seventh century the Tibetan King Songtsen Gampo unified the tribes on the Qinghai-Tibet plateau and established the Tubo Dynasty. King Songtsen Gampo married Princess Wencheng of the Tang Dynasty in 641, after which the Tang emperor conferred on him the titles of "Imperial Son-in-Law Governor," "West Sea Prince," and "Treasured Prince."

In the year 710, Princess Jincheng of the Tang Dynasty also went as a bride to Tibet.

Between 705 and 821 the Tang court and Tubo (Tibet) held eight conferences to pledge peaceful relations between the two sides. The last one produced what is known in history as "The Maternal Uncle-Nephew Alliance." The declaration of the Alliance stated in part: "The Tang Emperor and the Tibetan King, as maternal uncle and nephew, have met and agreed to become allied as one. They pledge to maintain the alliance forever, so that it may be witnessed and praised by the ecclesiastical and secular communities for generations to come."

With the development of political relations, came the growth of economic and cultural exchanges between the Tang Dynasty and Tubo. This laid down a foundation for the later establishment of a unified state.

Marriage relations between the Tang dynasty and the Tubo rulers.

与诸臧庶共处时,　　　　我之行仪应如何。”
如此挥泪而作叮嘱。
帝父亦以爱怜温语愍之曰:

“如我眼目汝娇女,	所谓吐蕃有雪地,
胜境钟灵有如是。	雪山天然宝塔形,
四湖犹若玉曼达[357],	奇异金花开遍处,
清凉美如无量宫。	四江横流木葱笼。
出产五谷并众宝,	牲畜遍野草如酥[358]。
如是希有胜妙处,	诸宝严饰为王宫。
人主牲普神所作,	真实大悲圣观音,
至为精明慈悲王,	除十恶业修十善,
黎民富庶受用丰,	功德无边天帝子,
智勇兼备臣菩萨,	如此胜地汝其行。
爱女积福所凭依,	有我所供本师像,
施主帝释天所造,	其质乃由十宝成,
毗首羯摩为工匠,	亲承如来赐开光。
如是无比如来像,	见、闻、念、触诚叩请,
佛说急速证阿像[359],	利乐源泉觉阿像[360],
舍此如含赛人心,	仍以赏赐我娇女。
诸种府库财帛藏,	众多宝物虽难备,
仍以赐赏我娇女。	告身文书金玉制,
经史典籍三谷六,	还有种种金玉饰,
以此赏赐我娇女。	诸种食物烹调法,
与及饮料配制方,	玉片鞍冀黄金鞍,
以此赏赐我娇女。	八狮子鸟织锦垫,
并绣枝叶宝篆文,	赐女能使王惊奇。
汉书告则经[361]三百,	能示休咎命运镜,
以此赏赐我觉。	工巧技艺制造术,
高超能令人称赞,	如此工艺六十法,
以此赏赐我娇女。	四百又四医方药,
四方、五诊、四论医典,	六医器械皆赐汝。
一世温暖锦缎罗,	具满各色作服饰,
凡二万匹赐与汝。	身材妙曼可爱儿,
善承人意诸女伴,	二十五名作侍女,
呼嗟,难忍分离娇女,	殷切教诲切记取,
为欲化度雪邦人,	汝之行仪应如是,
识见宜广行谨慎,	对内外事须明敏,
言语温和性善良,	恭敬赞普爱臣民,
知惭识愧行合矩。”	

The picture is reproduced from the Tibetan history book "The Records of the Tibetan Royal Lineage". It shows the Tang Emperor Tai Zong giving an image of Shakyamuni, jewelry, Buddhist scriptures, bookcases, classic works in 360 volumes to Princess Wencheng as her dowry. After marrying Princess Wencheng, King Songtsen Gampo sent groups of Tubo youths from noble families to Chang'an, capital of the Tang Dynasty, to study Chinese culture.

◄ King Songtsen Gampo, the founder of the Tubo Dynasty, sent envoys to the Tang capital city of Chang'an to seek marriage relations. In 641, Princess Wencheng went westward as a bride to Tubo. From then on, close relations were formed between the Tang Dynasty and Tubo. *The Audience,* a picture done by painter Yan Libén of the Tang Dynasty shows the Tang Emperor Tai Zong giving an audience to Gar Tongtsen, an envoy sent by King Songtsen Gampo to ask for the hand of a Tang princess in marriage.

The Tang Princess Jincheng went as a bride to Tuto in 710. She did her best to introduce the Tang culture to Tubo. According to *New History of the Tang Dynasty:* "The Tubo King sent envoys to welcome Princess Jincheng. The Emperor bestowed upon the Princess tens of thousands of bolts of silk and cloth, musicians, acrobats, all kinds of artisans, and a band of Qiuci musicians."

According to the *Old History of the Tang Dynasty,* "Having gone to Tibet, Princess Jincheng dispatched special envoys to the Tang court for a copy of each of the following books: the *Books of Poetry* (Mao Heng's version), *Book of Rites. Zuo Zhuan* (the famous commentary by Zuo Qiuming on *The Spring and Autumn Annals*), and *Selected Works* (a well-known selection noted for essays of elegant style dating from early centuries A. D.).

Eight conferences between Tang and Tubo to pledge peaceful relations.

In 821, the Tubo king sent envoys to request an alliance with the Tang court. The eighth alliance of the Tang and Tubo was concluded at Lhasa in 822. Liu Yuanding, the Minister of the Tang court, and the king of the Tubo concluded the alliance and took their solemn oath. The Uncle-Nephew Alliance Tablet was erected in 823.

The text of the Uncle-Nephew Alliance Tablet gives the history of the matrimonial alliance between the Tang and Tubo and states their determination of "keeping on the everlasting friendship between the uncle and nephew." "The Tang Emperor and the Tubo King as maternal uncle and nephew have met with agreement to become allied as one. They pledge to maintain the alliance forever, so that it may be witnessed and praised by ecclesiastical and secular communities for generations to come."

The picture shows the text engraved on the east side of the stone tablet.

Text on the west side of the Uncle-Nephew Alliance Tablet

大蕃神圣赞普可黎可足德赞与大唐文武孝德皇帝，商议社稷如一，（舅甥）二主，结立大和盟约，永无沦替，是以盟会节目，题之于碑也。

圣神赞普鹘提悉补野，化身下界，来主人间，为吐蕃大王。于雪山（高耸）之中央，大河奔流之源头，高原（净土），自天神而为人主，德泽流被，建成万世不朽之基业，创立至善之文法，睿哲鸿被，政事清明。圣神赞普，深诸韬略，外敌调伏，开疆拓土，誉盛莫比。自此"雍中"护持之王以后，南方之门（域）、天竺，西方之（大食），北方之突厥、涅牟（？）诸君长，莫不臣服圣神赞普，争相朝贡，俯首听命。东方有国曰唐，地极大海日出之处，与珞（瑜）、泥婆罗诸国迥异，教化德深，足与吐蕃并称。始初李氏建国之二十三年，王统一传，圣神赞普弃苏农赞与唐主太宗文武圣皇帝，叶同社稷如一家，于贞观朝，迎娶文成公主为赞普王妃；嗣后，圣神赞普弃隶蹜赞又与唐主三郎开元圣文显武皇帝，叶同社稷如一家，重申姻好，于景龙朝，复迎娶金城公主为赞普王妃，结成甥舅亲谊。中间边将开衅，弃好寻仇，兵争不已。当此忧危之际，仍于欢好之念，终未断绝，以彼此近邻而又素相亲厚，重寻甥舅之盟。父王圣神赞普弃德松赞陛下，睿智天成，教兴政举，普施鸿恩，泽被内外，遍及八荒。四方君长，率尔来臾，唐国宜属近亲，地接比邻，甥舅协和，叶同社稷如一，唐主神圣文武皇帝，结立大和盟约，旧恨消泯，再续新谊。此后，赞普甥传位一代，唐主舅又传三叶，嫌怨未生，欢好不绝，书翰通传，珍宝馈遗，络绎于途，然未遽结立大和盟约也。夫甥舅亲谊，协和如一，扫彼旧恨，弃其嫌隙，喜兵革之不作，惟亲好之是崇。我圣神赞普可黎可足德赞陛下，圣明睿哲，天神化现，恩施内外，威震四方，基业宏献，政令必行。乃与唐主文武孝德皇帝舅甥叶同社稷如一，结立大和盟约于唐京师西方之王会寺（？）前，时大蕃彝泰七年，大唐长庆元年，即阴铁牛年（辛丑）孟冬之月（十月）十日，登坛陟降，大唐主盟。续盟于吐蕃逻些东方之哲堆园，时大蕃彝泰八年，大唐长庆二年，即阳水虎年（壬寅）仲夏之月（五月）六日，登坛陟降，大蕃主盟。其立石于此为大蕃彝泰九年，大唐长庆三年，即阴水兔年（癸卯）仲春之月（二月）十四日事也。树碑之日，唐使太仆寺少卿杜载……等参与告成之礼，同一盟文之碑树于（唐之京师）。

（译自《唐蕃会盟碑》东侧纪会盟文藏文，参照王忠：《新唐书吐蕃传笺证》译文。）

Exchanges of emissaries between Tang and Tubo.

冊府元龜　卷九八〇　外臣部　通好　一五一五

少卿兼御史中丞持節充用立迴紇使其月以衛尉

少卿侯幼平兼御史中丞充入吐蕃告卹等使

元和四年正月命中官元文政往渤海充弔冊立使

七月吐蕃遣使來和好

五年五月吐蕃遣使論思熱來朝并歸鄭叔矩崔

泌之樞及叔矩男武延等一十三人叔矩會盟使崔

漢衡之從事泌渾瑊之從事貞元初吐蕃背盟所陷

凡二十餘年竟不屈節因及於蕃中至是請和故歸

其樞

冊府元龜　外臣部　卷之九百八十　十五

六月宰相與吐蕃使語中書令廳蕃使拜階下宰相

階還牢禮

七月以陝州大都督府左司馬兼通事舍人李銛為

鴻臚少卿攝御史中丞持節充入吐蕃使仍賜紫金

魚袋太子中舍人吳聿為丹王府長史兼侍御史為

之副

七年正月癸未以鴻臚卿張茂宣充人迴鶻使通事

舍人張賈副焉

二月吐蕃東道節度論詺都宰相尚綺心兒以書遺

鳳翔節度使李惟蘭惟蘭奏獻之

三月命宰臣於中書與吐蕃使議事

七月以京兆府功曹李泌為殿中侍御史太人朝雄

八年正月命內侍李重旻充渤海冊立宣慰使

副使

十一月黠戛明夷請歸其先侵牂牁之地

十一年二月授渤海國信以歸

五月命中使二人送迴鶻使歸國

十一月命正卿李誠兼御史中丞充入迴鶻使

十二年四月吐蕃以贊普卒來告已未以右衛將軍

烏重玼兼御史中丞弔贈吐蕃贊普使

冊府元龜　外臣部　卷之九百八十　十六

五月癸亥以右補闕段均為殿中侍御史充贈吐

蕃使

十三年三月渤海國遣使李繼常等二十六人來朝

十月鳳翔節度使鄭餘慶奏吐蕃遣使脩好

穆宗元和十五年即位八月乙亥命宰臣召吐蕃使

於中書議事十月命高品竇千乘使於吐蕃

十月庚午以太子中允張賈為太府少卿攝御史

中丞持節充入吐蕃答請和好使庚辰命宰臣召吐

蕃使於中書議事以鄔王府長史鄭同為太府少卿

兼御史中丞持節入吐蕃充答請和好使

In a period of 213 years beginning from 634 to 846, there were frequent friendly contacts between the Tang and Tubo, altogether 191 envoys were sent to or came from Tubo. The picture shows a record from *Ce Fu Yuan Gui* (a classical history book) about the Tang Emperor Muzong summoning the Tubo envoy for a talk and sending Gao Pingdou on a mission to Tubo.

In the 13th century

In the Yuan Dynasty Tibet Became an Administrative Region of China.

In the thirteenth century Temujin (Genghis Khan), who succeeded in subjugating other independent tribes and local forces, founded the Mongol Khanate. In 1247 Sakya Pandita, the chief of the Sakya Buddhist sect in Tibet, and his nephew Phagpa, conferred with the Mongol Prince Godan, grandson of Genghis khan, at Liangzhou (in present-day Gansu province) on problems concerning Tibet giving its allegiance to the Mongol Khanate. On his accession to the throne in 1260, Kublai Khan granted Phagpa the title of "Imperial Tutor" as well as a jade seal symbolizing the politico-religious power over Tibet, with which Phagpa was entrusted. This initiated the combination of temporal and spiritual authority in the Tibetan local regime. In 1271 Kublai Khan named his state the Yuan dynasty. In 1279 he unified China's entire territory. It was then that Tibet became an administrative region under the direct jurisdiction of the central government of China.

The Yuan Dynasty established the *Xuan Zheng Yuan* (Commission for Buddhist and Tibetan Affairs) in its central government to handle Buddhist affairs throughout China, including both the civil and military affairs of Tibet. It also set up a Pacification Commissioner's Offices in Tibet. Ü-Tsang was administratively divided into three regions with thirteen *wan hu* (meaning 10,000 households). The nomination of officials in Tibet had to be approved by the Yuan Court. The Yuan court carried out censuses, imposed taxes and levies and set up post-staging stations and monopoly markets in the Tibetan region.

Tibet pledged allegiance to the Yuan dynasty.

The Tibetan religious leader Sakya Pandita had a talk with Godan, grandson of Genghis Khan, at Liangzhou in 1247. In the same year Sakya Pandita sent a letter to all the ecclesiastical and secular leaders in Ü-Tsang and Ngari, saying: "the Mongol King's troops are innumerable, all the people of the world have pledged allegiance to him. He would share misfortunes and welfare with those who have sided with him, but he would not regard those as his subjects who overtly agree but covertly oppose him, and he would extinguish them in the end ..." He also talked about the administrative system the Mongol emperor had designed for Tibet.

Here is Sakya Pandita's letter, the whole text of the original letter is in *Sakya's Lineal prescriptions*.

ཁྱེར་ནས་ཟིང་ཕ་ཚོ་བཟུང་པར་གཏོང་པར་གདའ། རང་རེ་ཚོ་ཨང་བཟང་པོ་བྱ་
སྙམ་པའི་བསམ་ལ་ཡོད་ན་དེད་རང་གི་དཔོན་ག་ཀུན་ལ་འདགན་དོར་བཟོད་པོ་བཟུང་
ལ་ས་སྐྱ་པའི་མི་དང་འགྲོགས་ལ་ཕྱིན། འདབ་དོར་ནའི་ཚ་ཚིག་འདབ་ཟེར་
བའི་སྐོས་ཀྱིས། འདིར་ནས་ཀྱང་སྐོས་ཕྱེད། དེ་ནས་རང་ཕྱུལ་ཕོངས་ནས་རང་
གཞན་ཐམས་ཅད་ལ་ཕན་པར་བོད། ཁྱེར་ནས་ཀྱང་ད་ནེད་ནས་མི་བཏང་ནས་
འདི་ལྟར་བྱས་ན་ལེགས་བྱ་ན་ས་སྐོས་བསྐུལ་བ། ཁྱེད་རང་རྣམས་ཀྱི་ཀུང་དེ་
བཞིན་བྱེད་པའི་རིགས་སུ་མེད་པ་འདུག བསྐུལ་བའི་ཟེར་ལ་ཁྱེད་ར་དད་ཚོ་ཙོ་
ཟེར་ཉན་པ་ཅིག་འདོད་ལ་ཡིན་ནས། ཙེ་ཟེར་བ་ཡིན་ཨང་ས་མོ་ སྙིས་ས་སྐྱ་པ་
དོར་གསེས་ཏུ་སོང་བ་ཡིན་ནེ་དེད་ལ་ས་ཕན་ཟེར་བ་དེ་མི་ག་ཟུང་པར་ཞུ། འཆ་
བདག་ལས་གཟུ་གཉན་ཁ་ཉིད་བཟའ་ལ་ཕྱན་ནས་ཕོད་སྐུན་ཟླ་བ་ཐམས་ཅད་ལ་
ཕྱན་པའི་ཤྱིང་དུ་ཐོར་གསེབ་ཏུ་ཞོང་བ་ཡིན་ཏེ། ངས་ཙེ་ཟེར་ལ་ཞན་ན་ཕན་པར་
འདུག ཁྱིད་རྣམས་ཀྱིས་འདིའི་སྐྱལ་ཚུལ་མ་མཛོང་། ཕོས་ས་རྣམས་ལ་ཨིད་ཆེས་
པ་ཡིན་ཏུ་དགའི། དེའི་སྐྱོབས་ཀྱིས་ང་དུང་བཏབ་པར་ཞོར་སྐམ་སྐྱེ། བདེ་བའི་
འཕོ་ལ་སྐྱོ་བྱར་དུ་འདྲེ་མཆན་པ་ལུ་ཕྱེའི་འཕེན་གཤོན་ཚིག་བྱུང་ནས་དུས་ལ...
གཅན་གྱི་བྱ་དང་མི་ས་སོགས་པ་དོར་གསེབ་ཏུ་སོང་གིས་དགོས།   ཟེ་དེ་
ཤིགས་ཉིས་ཚི་བྱུང་ཨང་ང་ལ་འགྱོད་པ་མེད།   ས་མ་དཀོན་མཆོག་གི་བྱིན་རླབས་
དང་བགས་ཏེན་གྱིས་དུ་དུང་ཤིགས་པོ་ཞོན་བཟང་སྐྱེ། ཁྱེད་རང་རྣམས་ཀྱང་
དཀོན་མཆོག་ལ་གསོལ་བ་ཐོབ། རྒྱལ་པོ་ཏེད་ལ་སུ་དུང་ཨང་མི་འདུ་བའི་
ཕྱགས་ལ་བཏགས། དེའི་སྐྱོབས་ཀྱིས་རྒྱ་ཕོད། ཡུ་གུར། མི་ཉག་ལ་སོགས་པའི་
དགུ་བ་ཤེས་མི་ཆེན། ཡུལ་མི་གཅིག་ལ་པ་ཐམས་ཅད་ཀྱིས་དོ་མཆར་ཆེ་སྐྱ་ན་ས་
ཚེས་ཉན་པ་དང་གུས་པ་ཆེ་བ་འདུག དེ་འདིར་དོར་པ་རྣམས་ལ་དོར་གྱིས་ཞ་
འདི་ཕྱེ་སྟམ་པའི་རིགས་ལ་ས་དགོ། ཐམས་ཅད་ཀྱི་ཡུགས་ལ་བདགས་ནས་
བཟང་པོར་ཡོད་ཕས། ཟེ་ད་ཀྱི་ཕྱོགས་ནས་ཐམས་ཅད་སྐོ་བའི་བར་འཕྱགས་ཕས་

ཚིག འདབ་དོར་ལ་གསེར། དགལ། སྐྱང་པོ་ཆེ་ཨཚ་པ། སྤུ་ཏིག་དོག་པོ་
ཆེ་བ། མཚལ། བཙལ་ད། ར་དྲ། གི་ལིང་། སྤྲག་གཟིག་ལྱང་སུམ། སུམ།
ཕོད་སྐུམ། དྲུན་ཕྱག་འབཟང་པ། འདི་ན་དེ་ཚོ་དགལ་བར་འདུག སྐྱེ་ནོར་
ལ་འདིར་གཏགས་རྒྱོ་ཚི་ཨང་རང་རང་གི་ཡུལ་ན་གང་འཛང་གི་ནོར་རྫེ་རོང...
བས་ཚིག་པ་ཡིན། གསེར་ཡོད་ན་གང་འདིར་ཕོར་པར་འདུག་པས་དགོངས་
མཛོད། སང་ས་རྒྱལ་གྱི་བསྟན་པ་ཕྱོགས་འཕར་དགའ་དུ་རྒྱ་པར་ཀྱང་ཅ་མ། མན
ཕོ་ཞེ་ཞེ་པའི་གཟུང་ཕོག་གནང་བ་བཞིན་གཟང་གི་གྱ་ཐུ་ཕུ་སྐོ་ཏུ་མྱི་བདགི...
དང་བཅས་ན་སོགས་མ་སྐྱ་ཏེ་ཐམས་ཅད་ཀྱིས་མཆོང་ནས་ས་སོར་དགང་ནེ་མགུ་མི་
རང་ཞིང་ཡིད་སྐྱོ་མ་མཆོག་ཏུ་ཐོབ་ལ་པར་མཛད་པ་ཡིན་ན། ད་ལྟ་སྒྱི་སྐྱ་མ་
ཏོད་པའི་དུག་ཀྱི་ཐམས་ཅད་མཆྱིལ་པ་ལ་གཏིག་ལ་དེ་དགུ་པོ་འདུག་ཤུ་བར་དུ་
རྒྱལ་བའི་བསྟན་པ་དང་།   སེམས་ཅན་དཔལའ་དུ་མེད་ལ་སྒྱིད་ཉེང་སྐོ་ལ་བར་
མཛད་ནས།   མཐར་གཙུགས་ཀྱི་སྤྱི་བྱོའི་བ་ལི་ལུ་བཟ་བའི་རྒྱལ་སྐོ་དཔོན་
ཝ་ཙེ་བའི་གསུང་ལྱང་བཟོད་ན།   ལྱགས་ས་ལག་གི་དུ་སུ་གཞན་དོན་ལ་འཇུག
བའི་དུ་སུ་ན་སྣང་གི་སྐྱ་ལ་ལྱག་ཆེན་པོ་བཟ་བརྒྱུད་བྱུང་། ས་སྐྱར་ཕྱོ་ཆེ
བརྒྱུ་ཀྱི་ཉིན་པར་ས་གཡོལ་ས་ཆེན་པོ་བྱུང་། བདག་དེ་ཊ་ལྱ་རྫེ་རྗ་མཚན་ཞུས
ཕས། རྒྱལ་པའི་སྲས་ས་ཀུར་པ་ཆེན་པོ་རྣམས་གནན་དོན་ལ་འགྲོ་བའི་ལུས་ཡིན
ཙ་ཅག་ཀྱང་དེའི་རྗེས་སུ་འཇུག་པ་འདུ་གསུང་།   ཉི་ཀྱི་དགུའི་རྣམ་ཤྱེད་ཕ
ཕོང་སྐྱེའི་ལྱགས་སྐྱ་ལག་ག་དུངས་མི་ཞང་པ་སྐྱོག་པའི་རྒྱལ་པོ་མཛོར་སྐུམ་དུ་ཕྲོད།
སྐྱ་མ་དྲག་དྲང་པོ་ཞལ་གཅིག་ལ་ཕྱག་གཉིས་པ་ཕྱོན་ནས་ ཁྱིད་ཀྱིས་སྐོ་ཤུ...
གསང་ས་ནས་བདག་ གིས་སྐོ་ས་ཐུ།   ཕོ་རང་གི་དུ་སུ་སྐྱེད་ར་གཟིགས
དཔང་ཞལ་བཟ་གཅིག་ཕུ་ཕོས་ཀྱི་རྣབས་མཛོད་པའི་སྐྱང་བ་བྱུང་།   སྒྱོས་ཕུལ
གསང་ས་ནས་བདག་གིས་ཕུལ།   ལྱོན་དུ་ག་ག་ཀྱི་ཊ་ལ་བའི་ཡུ་ཚེ་དུ་ག་ཀྱི་ཐེན་ཊ་
ཚིགས་བཟགས། བདགྱི་དྲུང་ཕུ་ན་ཡོད་པར་ཟུ་ཕང་ག་གི་རང་ན་རྣམ་རྒྱལ་མཚོང་ར་

The seal of Prince Palen. Chakna Dorje accompanied Sakya Pandita to Liangzhou in 1247 and then stayed there. Kublai granted him the title of "Prince Palen" and a gold seal of authority and married Princess Mekhadun to him. He was the first Tibetan recipient of the title of "prince".

The Yuan emperor Shizu (Kublai Khan) had an audience with Phagpa, leader of the Sakya sect of the Tibetan Buddhism, on Mt. Liupan (in modern Ningxia Hui Autonomous Region) in 1251. He invested Phagpa with the title of "State Tutor" in 1260 and put him in charge of the *Zong* *Zhi Yuan*, thus, making him one of the high-ranking officials of the central regime.

The picture shows a mural in the Tashil-hunpo monastery in Shigatse depicting Phagpa meeting Kublai.

The jade axe bestowed on Phagpa by Kublai Khan.

The sword bestowed on Chakna Dorje by Kublai.

The Yuan dynasty conducted a census and set up poststage stations in Tibet.

In 1268, the Yuan Emperor Shizu (Kublai Khan) sent Akon, Miling and other officials to carry out an accurate census in Tibet. Their investigation played a decisive role in the later establishment of the local Tibetan administrative system and the setting up of a series of post-staging stations. The picture is the record in the *History of the Yuan Dynasty* about the census in Tibet.

清 查 户 口

阿衮（ཨ་ཀོན）弥林（མི་གླིང）来到乌思、藏，欲清查民户（མི་སེ）土地之数。① 以户（དུད）为计算单位。他若不属于万户、千户之农民及牧民（འབྲོག་འབྲེག），吐蕃上部之纳里速古鲁孙及南方各地面均不在清查之列。所清查者乌思、藏及其他万户所属户数如下：

拉堆南部（ལ་སྟོད་ལྷོ）〔万户〕，一千九百九十户；

拉堆北部（ལ་སྟོད་བྱང）〔万户〕，二千二百五十户；

出密（ཆུ་མིག）万户，三千零三户；

沙鲁（ཞ་ལུ）万户，三千八百九十二户。

其次则为绛卓（བྱང་འབྲོག）、雅卓万户（ཡར་འབྲོག）下设"雷卜"十六个，共计七百五十户。

乌思（前藏）民户数如下：

必里公（འབྲི་གུང，即止贡）合农民及收民共计三千六百三十户；搽里八（ཚལ་པ，即蔡巴）三千七百户；伯木古鲁巴（ཕག་མོ་གྲུ་པ，即帕竹）二千四百三十八户；牙里不藏思八（གཡའ་བཟངས་པ，即亚桑巴）三千户；加麻瓦（རྒྱ་མ་བ）札由瓦（བྱ་ཡུལ་བ）共五千九百户而各有其半；思答笼刺（སྟག་ལུང，即达垅）五百户；益以拉竹（ལྷ་འབྲེག）等处散居者千四百户。此为乌思藏清查户口之始。②

（译自《五世达赖喇嘛传》，拉萨版，20—21叶。）

注：①元世祖忽必烈派官赴乌思、藏地方清查户口，事在前 至元五年戊辰（1268年）。
②据八思巴1252年所写的两封书信，蒙哥在汗位时已派 人到乌思藏清查户口，并由八思巴派人协助。

The Yuan dynasty established administrative organs and appointed officials in Tibet.

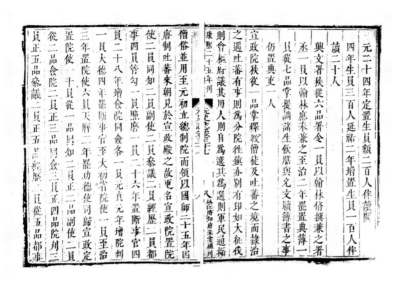

The Yuan Emperor Shizu (Kublai Khan) set up *Zong Zhi Yuan* in the central government in 1264. It was an institution in charge of Buddhist affairs across the country and the Tibetan local administrative affairs. In 1288 it was renamed as *Xuan Zheng Yuan* (Commission for Buddhist and Tibetan Affairs).

The picture shows the record in the *History of the Yuan Dynasty* about the central government setting up the *Xuan Zheng Yuan.*

The Yuan Emperor Shizu (Kublai Khan) established three Offices of the Pacification Commission and Chief Military Command in Ü-Tsang and Ngari Korsum and set up thirteen Brigades (*wan-hu fu,* a standard military unit theoretically comprising 10,000 soldiers under a Brigade Commander, *wan-hu*). The Emperor appointed Sakya the head of the thirteen Brigades and installed a *Ponchen* (military commander) in Sakya to take charge of the thirteen Brigades. All the *Ponchens* and Brigade Commanders were nominated by the Imperial Preceptor and appointed by the central authorities. Tibet became officially an administrative region of China. The local Tibetan regime based on an amalgamation of temporal and spiritual government had come into being ever since.

The picture shows the record in the *History of the Yuan Dynasty* about the establishment of the three Offices of Pacification Commission and Chief Military Command and the thirteen Brigades.

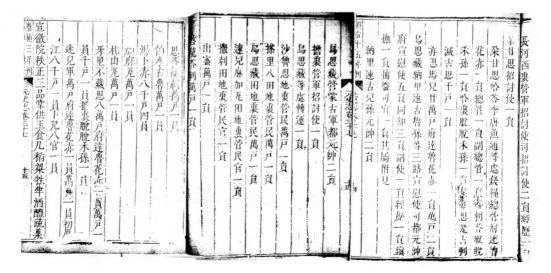

1. Phagpa Lodro Gyaltsen (vPhags-pa blo-gros rgyal-mtshan, 1235-1280), State Tutor from 1260 to 1270, Imperial Tutor to the Yuan dynasty emperor Shizu (Kublai) from 1270 to 1280.

2. Rinchen Gyaltsen (Rin-chen rgyal-mtshan, 1238-1279), Imperial Tutor to the Yuan dynasty emperor Shizu (Kublai) during 1276-1279.

3. Dharmapala (Dharma pa-la rakashi-ta, 1269-1287), son of Chakna Dorje, who was phagpa's brother; Imperial Tutor to the Yuan dynasty emperor Shizu (Kublai) during 1281-1286.

4. Yeshe Rinchen (Ye-shes rin-chen, 1249-1295), Phagpa's disciple, Imperial Tutor to the Yuan dynasty emperor Shizu (Kublai) during 1286-1291.

5. Drakpa Odser (Grags-pa vod-zer, 1246-1303), Phagpa's personal attendant, Imperial Tutor to Yuan emperor Shizu (Kublai) and Yuan emperor Cheng Zong (Timur) during 1291-1303.

6. Richen Gyaltsen (Rin-chen rgyal-mtshan, 1257-1305), younger brother of the fourth Imperial Tutor Yeshe Rinchen. He was appointed by Yuan emperor Shizu (Kublai) to be abbot of the Sakya Shitog Lhadrang, and became the Imperial Tutor of Yuan emperor Cheng Zong (Timur) from 1303 to 1305.

7. Sengye Pal (Sangs-rgyas dpal, 1267-1314), nephew of the fifth Imperial Tutor Drakpa Odser. He was once the abbot of the Sakya Monastery and then the Imperial Tutor to the Yuan emperors Cheng Zong (Timur), Wu Zong (Khaissan) and Ren Zong (Ayurbadrabal).

8. Kunga Lodro Gyaltsen Palzangpo (Kun-dgar blo-gros rgyal-mtshan dpal-bzang-po, 1299-1327), Phagpa's grand-nephew, Imperial Tutor to the Yuan emperors Ren Zong (Ayurbad-rabal), Ying Zong (Shoodbal) and Tai Ding Di (Yesuntemur).

9. Wangchuk Gyaltsen (dbang-phyug rgyal-mtshan), Imperial Tutor to Tai Ding Di (Yesuntemur) from 1323 through 1325 according to the "Section on Famous Buddhist Monks and Taoist Priests" in the *History of the Yuan Dynasty*. However, there is no such record in Tibetan historical documents. He probably acted as a deputy for the eighth Imperial Tutor, Kunga Lodro Gyaltsen Palzangpo, when the latter was away from Beijing.

10. Kunga Legpa Jungne Gyaltsen Palzangpo (Kun-dgav legs-pavi vbyung-gnas rgyal-mtshan dpal-bzang-po, 1308-1341), Phagpa's grand-nephew, Imperial Tutor to Yuan emperor Tai Ding Di (Yesuntemur) during 1328-1329.

11. Rinchen Drashi (Rin-chen bkra-shis), Imperial Tutor from 1329 to 1332. He was the last Imperial Tutor recorded in the "Section of Famous Buddhist Monks and Taoist Priests" in the *History of the Yuan Dynasty*. But there are no records of him in Tibetan historical documents. Probably he was also an acting Imperial Tutor.

12. Kunga Gyaltsen Palzangpo (Kun-dgav rgyai-mtshan dpal-bzang-po, 1310-1358), Phagpa's grand-nephew, Imperial Tutor to Yuan emperor Shun Di (Togontemur).

13. Lachen Sonam Lodro (bla-chen bsod-nams blo-gros, 1332-1362), Phagpa's great grand-nephew. There are no records about him in Chinese historical documents. *Sakya's Lineal Description* (*Sa-skya dung-rabs*) says he was appointed Imperial Tutor. It seems that he was the Imperial Tutor to Shun Di (Togontemur) from 1358 to 1362.

14. Namgyal Palzangpo (rnam-rgyal dpal-bzang-po), appointed as Imperial Tutor after 1362 by the end of the Yuan dynasty. At the beginning of the Ming dynasty, he was appointed as "State Tutor of Prosperous Buddhist Treasure", according to Chinese historical records.

Imperial Tutor was an important official in the central government of the Yuan Dynasty. From 1270 when Phagpa was made the first Imperial Tutor to the fall of the Yuan Dynasty, every emperor had his own Imperial Tutor. There were altogether fourteen Imperial Tutors. The above is a table of their names.

From the 14th to the 17th century

The Ming Imperial Court's Administration of Tibet

In the Ming Dynasty the policy towards Tibet mainly continued that of the previous Yuan Dynasty. The governorship for Ü-Tsang and a Marshal's Headquarters were created. The system of official posts in Tibet ranking from commanders, commissioners to *wan hu, qian hu,* and *bai hu* was improved. Officials in Tibet were appointed by the central government. In carrying out a pacificatory policy, the Ming Dynasty granted various new offices and titles of honor to officials and dignitaries in the Tibetan areas. Thus the title of "Prince of Dharma" was granted to Khon Drakpa of the Sakya sect, "Prince of Great Treasure" to Karma Lama of the Kagyupa sect, "Prince of the Western Deities and Grand Imperial Tutor" and later "The Great Compassionate Prince of the Dharma" to Shakya Yeshe of the Gelugpa (Yellow-Hat) sect. Among many other titles of honor were those of "Initiation State Tutor," "Promotion Prince of Virtue," "Guardian Prince of the Doctrine," "Propagation Prince of the Doctrine."

The tribute-paying system was also an important policy in regard to Tibet. It not only showed Tibet's subordination to the Ming central government, but also stimulated Tibet's economic and cultural development and exchanges with central China.

The Ming dynasty carried on the institutions set up by the Yuan in Tibet and adjusted administrative apparatus for the Tibetan areas.

The Ming court set up *Xi'an* Branch Regional Military Commission in Hezhou (modern Linxia County in Gansu Province) in charge of Ü-Tsang, Dokham and Hezhou commanderies to govern all the Tibetan areas. Then the Ü-Tsang commandery became the Ü-Tsang Branch Regional Military Commission, whose jurisdiction covered Tibet.

This picture is the record in the *History of the Ming Dynasty* about the administrative and military apparatus of Tibet.

The central government of the Ming dynasty held judicial power.

Tibetan local officials would be punished by the Ming court when they violated the law.

Reproduction from *the Imperial Records of the Ming Dynasty*, the main point of which is as follows.

In 1431 Liu Zhao, vice commissioner-in-chief in Hezhou reported to the emperor: "Ashgi, a battalion chief of the Tibetan Rosnang tribe was murdered by his younger brother Gongkar, who seized his land. After interrogation the murderer admitted his guilt. I think that he should be beheaded."

The emperor replied: "To murder one's brother is not a common crime. The murderer must be beheaded and his head be exhibited to the public so that the people in the borderland may know the law should be observed."

Carrying out a pacificatory policy, the Ming dynasty granted various new offices and titles of honor to officials and dignitaries as well as the influential religious leaders in Tibetan areas. The tribute-paying system encouraged trade.

In 1406 Ming emperor Chengzu conferred on Drakpa Gyaltsen, Grand Lama of Phagmo Drupa regime of the Kagyu order, the title of "Prince of Persuasion (*Chanhua*)." This is the gold seal of authority bestowed on Drakpa Gyeltsen by the emperor.

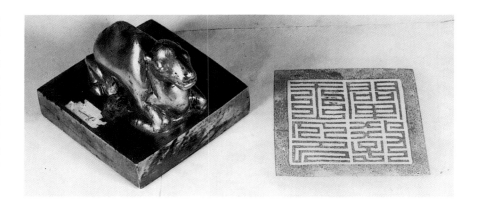

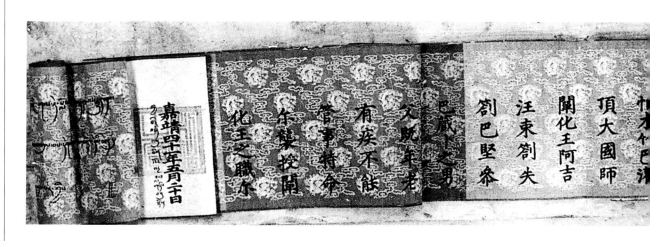

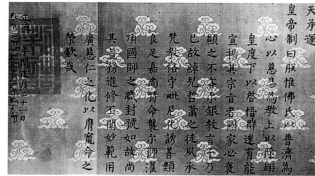

In 1466, Ming emperor Xianzong bestowed gifts on Karmapa, Great Treasure Prince of Dharma of Ü-Tsang. This is the imperial edict for the bestowal.

The Ming court set up eight "Princes of Dharma" and "Princes," further established the system of monk officials and granted various honorific titles such as "Prince of Western Heaven," "Grand State Tutor," and "State Tutor."

Here the picture shows an imperial edict issued by the Ming emperor Shi Zong in the 11th year of the Jiajing reign (1562), which reads: "Drakpa Drashi Gyaltsen is the son of Ngagi Wangchu Drashi Drakpa Gyaltsen Palsanpo, Imperial Initiation Master and Prince *Chanhua* of Phagmo Drupa in Ü-Tsang. Since your father is too old and sick to handle administrative affairs, I order you to inherit the title and position of Prince *Chanhua*."

The picture shows an imperial edict issued by the Ming emperor Wu Zong in the second year of Zhengde reign period (1507), which reads: "The purpose of Buddhism is to save all beings, and it is merciful and compassionate. So the state always encourage and reward those who can propagate the doctrine of Buddhism. You, Yonten Rinchen are the disciple of Dorje, are well versed in Buddhist philosophy, have observed strictly the monastic disciplines and know very well how to educate people —all this is worthy of high praise. Therefore I order you to inherit the title and position of the State Tutor of Initiation."

23

In carrying out a policy of pacification, the Ming Dynasty granted various offices and honorific titles to political and religious leaders in the Tibetan areas. Tribute-paying and bestowing were an important measure of the policy.

Reproduction from the *Imperial Records of the Ming Dynasty*, which shows the Ming court stipulated that the Tibetan monks of Ü-Tsang should pay tributes to the emperor every three years.

可○戊辰定烏思藏番僧三年一貢例禮部奏宣德正統間番

遠近分撥官軍之運廉民不困於凶年而國用亦無所損矣制

廣募商人於淮安徐州德州水次舍分中納俟未歲斟酌的道里

不足請以淮浙等處官鹽二百七十萬引酌量米價定擬則例

南畿運京儲四百餘萬石今罹災傷優免歲衆運必有

部言鎮江浙江諸處旱潦相繼以賑濟然國家財賦仰給東

府庫供無益之遠夷請會官議處可以經久長行者從之○戶

而使臣來者三百六十餘人皆欲給賞今歲饑民困以有限之

地面遣使臣於的馬黑麻等來貢禮部議哈審貢馬繞二十疋

寅發銀四萬兩賑濟鳳陽徐州饑民從戶部請也○丁卯哈審

秩滿命陞俸一級再任三年以巡撫都御史王恕奏保也○丙

未嘗救鄉所議良是其著為令○湖廣襄陽府知府干璠九年

From the 17th to the 20th century
The Qing Imperial Court Improving the Administration of Tibet

Under the succeeding Qing dynasty, the central government of China further strengthened its administration of Tibet. In 1652 the fifth Dalai Lama paid his respects in Beijing to the emperor, who, in the following year, granted him the title of "Buddha of Great Compassion in the West, Leader of the Buddhist Faith Beneath the Sky, Holder of the Vajra, the Dalai Lama" and a certificate on sheets of gold inscribed and a gold seal of authority. In 1713 the fifth Panchen Lama was granted the title of "Panchen Erdeni" as well as gold seal and certificate on sheets of gold. From that time on, the Qing central government officially recognized the political and religious status and powers of the Dalai and Panchen Lamas.

In 1727 the Qing Dynasty began to appoint Grand Minister Residents of Tibet.

In 1751 the *Kashag*—the administrative council of the Tibetan government composed of four ministers (*kalon*)—was officially set up in Tibet.

In 1793 the Qing central government laid down "The Twenty-nine-Article Ordinance for the More Effective Governing of Tibet," comprising a series of regulations concerning the management of personnel, administrative, financial, military and foreign affairs in Tibet. The ordinance established the institution of "Drawing Lots from the Golden Urn." This prescribed that the incarnation of the Dalai Lama, the Panchen Erdeni and other Living Buddhas of the Yellow-Hat sect was subject to the supervision and authorization by the central government of China.

The Qing dynasty conferred titles of honor on the Dalai and the Panchen.

In 1578, Altan Khan conferred on the Third Dalai Lama an honorific title of "All-Knowing Vajra-Holder, the Dalai Lama" ("Dalai" meaning "ocean" in Mongolian and "Lama" meaning "Superior master" in Tibetan). This is the origin of the title of "Dalai Lama." In 1653, the Qing dynasty Emperor Shunzhi granted the Fifth Dalai Lama the title of "Buddha of Great Compassion in the West, leader of the Buddhist Faith Beneath the Sky, All-Knowing Vajra-Holder, Dalai Lama" as well as a title-conferring golden album and a gold seal of authority inscribed in the Manchu, Chinese, Mongolian and Tibetan languages. From then on the title of "Dalai Lama" was authorized by the Qing court.

Here is the record from the *Imperial Records of the Qing Dynasty* about conferring the title.

Reproduction of the gold-gilt album inscribed with the Qing emperor Daoguang's order in 1839 conferring recognition to the Eleventh Dalai Lama.

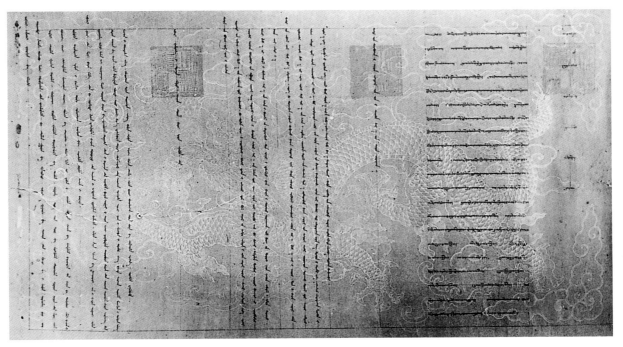

The title of "Panchen Erdeni" was granted by the Qing Emperor Kangxi to the Fifth Panchen Lama in 1713. The title has been maintained until now.

Pictured here is the imperial edict for conferring the title upon the Sixth Panchen Lama.

Reproduction of the golden album bestowed in 1838 by the Qing emperor Daoguang upon the Seventh Panchen Erdeni.

The institution of "drawing lots from the golden urn" prescribed by the Qing dynasty in 1793 for the confirmation of reincarnation of the Dalai Lama.

The well-known *Twenty-nine-Article Ordinance for the More Efficient Governing of Tibet* laid down by the Qing court in 1793, prescribed the institution of the "Golden Urn" to determine the succession of the Dalai Lama, Panchen Erdeni and other high-ranking Tibetan and Mongolian incarnate Lamas of the Yellow-Hat sect. The golden urn for the incarnation-confirming ceremony was specially made. Thereafter, the official confirmation of the Dalai Lama was subject to authorization by the central government.

Here is the Golden Urn used for the incarnation-confirming ceremony in Tibet.

The Qing court instituted the office of Grand Minister Residents of Tibet.

In 1727, owing to internal discord of Tibet, the Grand Ministers of the Deliberative Council requested the emperor to give instructions to the Dalai Lama, Khangchennas, Ngabopa and others to handle affairs in cooperation. The emperor approved their request and sent a minister with an imperial edict to instruct these personages to be friendly to each other. Afterwards. Sengge, Academician of the Grand Secretariat, and Mala, Vice Commander-in-chief, were sent by the Qing court to Tibet as full and deputy Grand Minister Residents of Tibet. Their term of office was three years.

Pictured here is the text from the *Imperial Records of the Qing Dynasty* about the establishment of the office of Grand Minister Residents of Tibet.

Letter submitted by Sakya Monastery to the Grand Minister Resident of Tibet in the Qianlong reign asking for the pay and provision for the Qing troops who were at war with the Gurkhas.

A report about civil disputes, submitted by a leader of Sakya sect of the Tibetan Buddhism to the Grand Minister Resident of Tibet. It reads: "According to the emperor's instructions and for the benefit of the Buddhist adherents, we have specially gone there on a tour of inspection... Here I ask you for permission to summon the persons concerned and to send people to go there to distinguish right from wrong and then decide the case according to the law."

The Tibetan local government (Kashag) was established by the order of the Qing emperor of China.

In 1721, after suppressing a rebellion in Tibet, the Qing court abolished the title of Depa (the top administrator, who had centralized power in Tibet), and replaced him with four Kalons, who should jointly handle administrative affairs. In 1751 the Qing court established the *Kashag* (local government of Tibet).

Reproduced here is a passage from the *Imperial Records of the Qing Dynasty*: "general-governor Celeng is ordered to promote virtuous and able men according to traditional institutions and establish four Kalons, who will jointly handle administrative affairs of Tibet."

清實錄 乾隆十六年四月上

眼內布隆贊雙目失明難以復加錄用其策
布騰布隆贊三人俱藏內大族素為番眾所
達餘係扎薩克吉棄凌旺扎勒色玉特色
加訪察知舊例噶隆本屬四人一條公班第
地噶隆多立敷人以分其勢隨就本屬藏第
俱悉○四川總督策楞奏前令將本地方密
帶挨查并咨會班第等一體查察得旨覽奏
請即駐爐地委泰寧協副將前往察木多一
甫經到口又復轉回恐番性多疑造言驚擾
行抵打箭爐地方去察木多二千五百餘里
兩日因各塘遠近不一故具報參差臣等已
人傳示各番不得驚擾漢人斷絕站路僅一
來文書并殺塘兵嗣達賴喇嘛公班第達差
沙格巴商圖報復圖通司岡令各喋巴阻往
特那木札勒被誅之後羅布藏扎什與白隆
收至始於何時一節查十月十三日珠爾默
公文等件事定後俱送交糧務通判常明查
絕外麥陳世庚處致有沈擱前項火票遞到

七五

駐藏大臣遵其指示而行爾等其感恩宣力
互相瞻顧遇有緊要事務稟知達賴喇嘛與
力黽勉供職勿存私意致生猜疑勿分彼此
事爾等當感戴朕恩尊敬達賴喇嘛和衷協
揀選賢能仍照舊例分設噶隆四員公同辦
靜噶隆事務不可一人專辦特令總督策楞
圖因此駐藏大臣將伊正法令藏內已經平
事專擅不與眾噶隆商議負恩任性潛懷異
務原係噶隆四人至珠爾默特那木札勒諸
西方佛教演經法從前供養喇嘛一切
西藏廣興黃教為清淨善地達賴喇嘛掌管
玉特色布騰扎薩克喇嘛尼瑪嘉木燦等曰
噶隆公班第達扎薩克台棄凌旺扎勒色
薩克喇嘛職銜放為噶隆公同辦事報可諭
嘛尼瑪嘉木燦明白可信臣等擬請給予扎
據達賴喇嘛以番眾不能深曉黃教係眾喇
此任應請仍放為噶隆至布隆贊所遺之缺
凌旺扎勒色玉特色布騰皆老成明白可勝

31

The Qing government prescribed a local standing army system in Tibet.

During the period between the disintegration of the Tubo dynasty and the late 18th century, there was never a standing army in Ü-Tsang. Soldiers were conscripted to perform military *ula* (corvèe). With the approval of the emperor of China. Qianlong, General Fu Kang'an proposed in 1792 that standing army of three thousand men should be built, that all officers be appointed by the Grand Minister Resident of Tibet conjointly with the Dalai and that the army should be inspected regularly by them both. The establishment of a standing army of Tibet was then stipulated by the Imperial Ordinance for the More Effective Governing of Tibet in 1793. This is a record of this in the *Imperial Records of the Gurkha Invasions.*

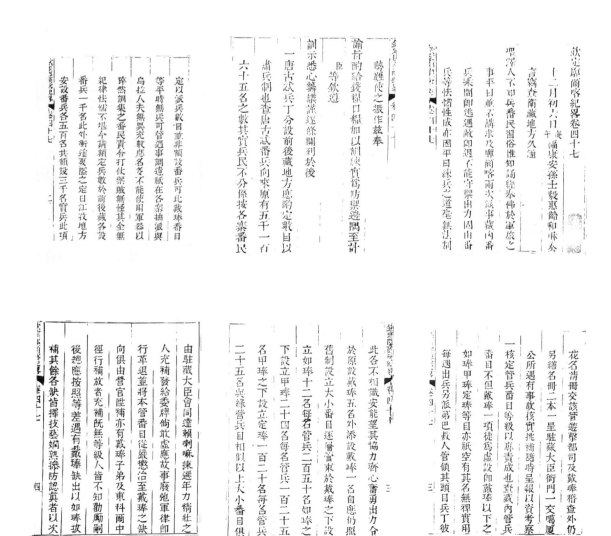

Silver coins were minted in Tibet under the supervision of the Qing central government.

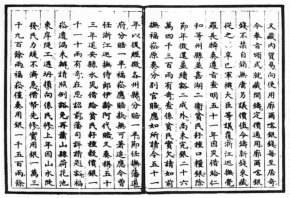
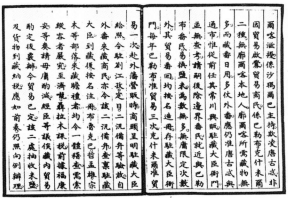

In 1791, the Qing court decreed the setting of a mint for Tibetan silver coins. Pictured here is a passage from the *Imperial Records of the Qing Dynasty*: "By the emperor's order, the minting of coins has begun in Tibet and the rates of exchange for other currencies have been fixed. The Gurkha silver coins shall be withdrawn from circulation."

Official document given by the Grand Minister Resident of Tibet and the imperial envoy to *kalons* about the circulation of silver coins. The document quoted a remark in the imperial edict as follows: "The Chinese officials and *kalons* are ordered to have a supervision of the minting of Tibetan silver coins stamped with the words *Qianlong Baozang* (Emperor Qianlong's Treasury), which shall be of pure Han silver and contains no impurities."

The *Twenty-nine-Article Ordinance for the More Efficient Governing of Tibet* promoulgated in 1793 prescribed the minting of Tibetan silver coins stamped with the characters "Qianlong Baozang" (Emperor Qianlong's Treasury).

Tibetan silver coins stamped with the characters "Qianlong Baozang", "Jiaqing Baozang" (Emperor Jiaqing's Treasury) and "Daoguang Baozang" (Emperor Daoguang's Treasury), minted under the supervision of the Grand Minister Residents of Tibet.

33

Imperial Ordinance for the More Effective Governing of Tibet

The Qing dynasty issued and enforced in 1793 the *Imperial Ordinance for the More Effective Governing of Tibet.* The ordinance comprised a series of regulations on the management of official personnel and administrative, financial, military and foreign affairs in Tibet. It served to institutionalize the administration, through which the central government of the Qing dynasty exercised its sovereignty over Tibet.

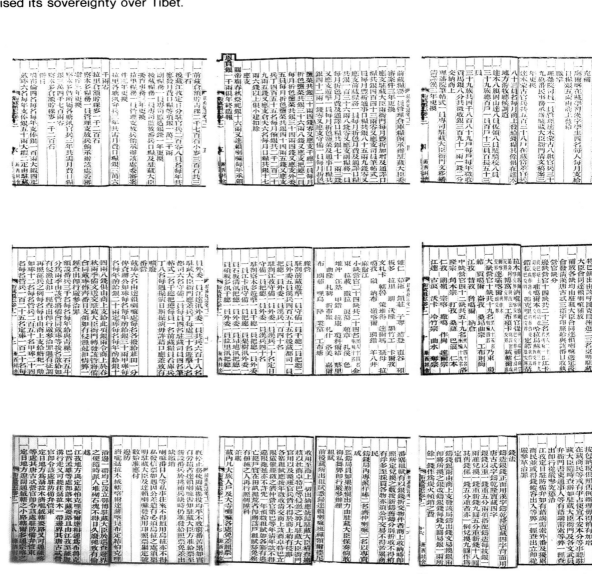

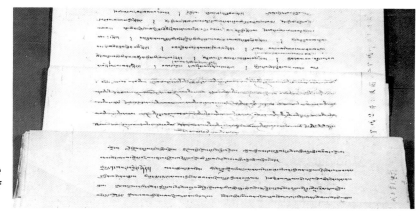

Imperial Ordinance for the More Effective Governing of Tibet

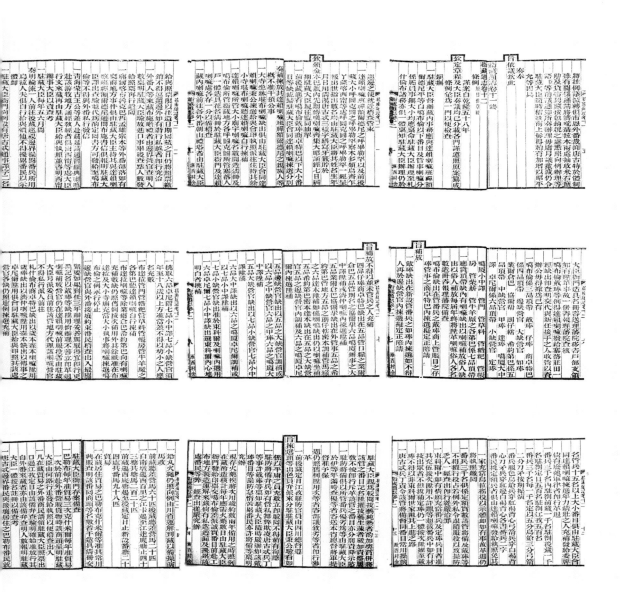

From 1912 to 1949
The Nationalist Government Safeguards China's Sovereignty over Tibet

In 1912, after the founding of the Republic of China, the central government termed itself a republic of five nationalities —Han, Manchu, Mongolian, Hui, and Tibetan—with a unified territory. The Provisional Constitution of the Republic of China stipulated: "The territories of the Republic of China include twenty-two provinces as well as Inner and Outer Mongolias, Tibet, and Qinghai." In 1912, the restoration of the title of the 13th Dalai Lama "The Loyally Submissive Vicegerent, Great, Good, Self-Existent Buddha of Western Heaven" was decreed by the president of the Republic of China.

In 1913 the title "Zhizhong Chanhua" (the Most Loyal Propagator) was conferred on the Panchen Lama. In 1929 the Nationalist Government of China established its Commission for Mongolian and Tibetan Affairs to strengthen the administration of Mongolia and Tibet. In 1934 the Tibetan office of the Commission for Mongolian and Tibetan Affairs was established. In 1931, 1936 and 1946 a number of Tibetan monks and lay officials were elected as delegates to the National Congress. The 9th Panchen and other prominent personages took office under the central government of China.

The title of "Great Master of infinite Wisdom, Defender of the Nation and Propagator of the Doctrine" conferred on the Panchen Erdeni by the Nationalist Government in 1931.

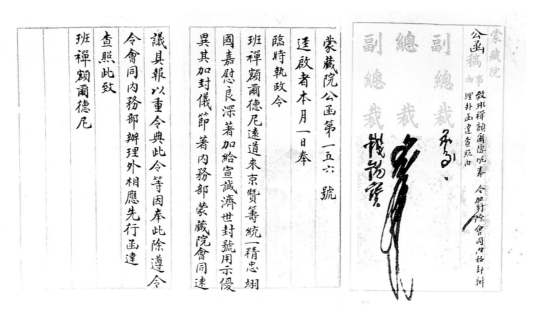

The republic of five nationalities founded in 1911, expressing the unity of the territory of China.

The Provisional Constitution of the Republic of China was promulgated on March 11, 1912. Its preamble stipulated: "The territory of the Republic of China includes twenty-two provinces as well as Inner and Outer Mongolias, Tibet, and Qinghai."

Reproduced here is a quotation from the *Provisional Constitution of the Republic of China* collected in the *Compilation of Chinese Constitutions.*

青海．

第二章 人 民

第五条 中华民国人民，一律平等，无种族、阶级、宗教之区别。

第三章 参议院

第十八条 参议员，每行省、内蒙古、外蒙古、西藏，各选派五人，青海选派一人，其选派方法，由各地方自定之。参议院会议时，每参议员有一表决权。

（《中国宪法类编》下编，页366,367。）

第一节 辛亥革命后，民国政府宣布实行五族共和，宣慰西藏地方

一、民国政府宣告民族统一，领土统一

孙总统宣言书

（1912年1月）

（前略）国家之本，在于人民，合汉、满、蒙、回、藏诸地为一国，则合汉、满、蒙、回、藏诸族为一人，是曰民族之统一。武汉首义，十数行省先后独立，所谓独立，对于清廷为脱离，对于各省为联合。蒙古、西藏，意亦同此，行动既一，决无歧趋，枢机成于中央，斯经纬周于四至，是曰领土之统一。

（《东方杂志》第八卷，第十号。）

中华民国临时约法（摘录）

（中华民国元年三月十一日公布）

第一章 总纲

第三条 中华民国领土，为二十二行省，内外蒙古，西藏，

国民政府行政院报告（摘录）

（前略）迨至北伐告成，国府于（民国）十八年（三月）成立蒙藏委员会。对蒙第一要务即在如何扶除中央与西藏之隔膜。受于十九年派北平雍和宫扎萨喇嘛贡觉仲尼携稀杂笔画件赴藏慰问达赖，达赖因受感召，乃有驻京代表之置，时尼泊尔尔与西藏发生战事，中央遂令西藏，复派蒙藏委员会参事巴文峻前往宣慰，借以调解，故事既息，西藏当局曾通息中央亦示感激之意，藏事至此始有转机。二十年蒙藏委员会复派该会专门委员关冏（国）梁父子入藏，宣达中央德意。……

（国民政府行政院档案。）

二、九世班禅坚持维护祖国领土完整和国家统一的爱国立场

班禅驻京办事处成立宣言①

（1929年1月）

最亲爱之中华民国五族同胞均鉴，中华民国，分崩忧乱十七年，内受军阀之困扰，外遭列器之压迫，使五族同胞，各不相顾，甚至情形隔膜，痛痒莫关。西藏远处西陲，所受影响尤深，今赖全国统一，蒙华重光，青天白日旗帜之下，尚有重行相聚之日，亦为幸矣，原西藏之于中国，自汉唐以还，关系日深，清季更置官吏戍守，微诸历史与地理上之关系，西藏欲令中国两诉自主，实不可能，反之，中国失去西藏，亦犹车之失轮，故中藏关系，合则两利，分则俱伤，此一定之道也，当膺末民初之际，汉藏间方多数人为个人之利害关系，不眷大局，互相斗争，结果，达赖逃亡于印度，同时产生李鸿英派，纷党操权，致于强邻以侵略之机会，辛亥之役，尽逐在藏官吏，从此中藏猜悄，日趋恶化。帝国主义者，更从事其经济文化之侵略，一方面又纵恿西藏独立，嗾使进兵占领西藏，侵犯肝及、几抵川境，对于人民，间荷虐藏俩，奸淫掳掠，宣声过财，锒琴殺迢，此皆由于少数亲英派之作祟，彼挈既存中藏之关系，且不顾西藏本身之利益，自目安行，神人共愤，且常以武力压迫俩，勒索重相，戕害人民，此此涯藏之下，敢怒而不敢言，班禅晴此情形，悲痛已极，乃容结全藏僧侣之公议，牺牲一切，代表东下，所抱家旨，简单言之，不外三点，（一）西藏始终与中国合作，贯侧五族亲和，共同抵制强邻之侵略，（二）希望中国以民族平等之观念，扶助及领导西藏人民，使之能自决自治，（三）继续保护维持西藏之宗教，再进西欢光大佛学之真精神，以谋世界之和平，抵内地以后，转瞬六年，只因内乱绵延，中枢无主，班禅满腹苦衷，无门告述，今幸统一告成训政伊始，内部既已平靖，宜尽力于国防之巩固，中华民国，既为整个之国家，则孙中山先生所遗留之主义及政纲政策，须力求实现于整个之国土，且藏康青海，地广人稀，蕴藏万里矿藏丰富，若使中山先生之实业计划，如大有种乎国计民生，假使个人械救及政府限裁，纸顾旋于东让长江黄河三流域之间，不于边疆，仍用读诫，则内地藏由训政实现，亦非国家长治久安之计，即中国之国民革命，亦不能谓为成功也，是本此在京筹备成立，即本班禅东下宗旨，向政府报告接洽一切，更希金国同胞，群起注意藏事，不胜企祷之至，谨以此宣，作此宣言！

南京奇望街班禅办公处启

（蒙藏委员会档案。）

Declaration issued by the 9th Panchen Erdeni's Office in Nanjing upon its establishment in January 1929.

"Since the Tang Dynasty Tibet has established a close relationship with China. The Qing Dynasty sent troops to safeguard Tibet. In view of the historical and geographical relations it is impossible for Tibet to be independent of China. The same is true of China. Without Tibet, China is like a car without wheels. So it will benefit both of us to be united while separation will cause damage to both us... Now the Panchen Erdeni's Office in Nanjing is established in accordance with the purpose of Panchen's coming eastward to the central China, i.e., to consult with the central government. Furthermore, it is hoped that our fellow-countrymen will pay attention to Tibetan affairs. This is what we pray for and is why we make this declaration with all sincerity."

Restoration of the title of honor to the Dalai Lama

大总统恢复达赖喇嘛封号令

（1912年10月28日）

据前达赖喇嘛阿旺罗布藏吐布丹甲错济寨旺曲却勒朗结致蒙藏事务局总裁贡桑诺尔布函称：前因教务由京回藏，振兴藏务，竭力整顿。嗣以革去名号，暂居大吉岭。去冬川省事起，藏中至今未靖，意欲维持佛教，请转呈妥商等语。现在共和成立，五族一家，前达赖喇嘛诚心内向，从前误解自应捐释，应即复封为诚顺赞化西天大善自在佛，以期维持黄教，赞翊民国，同我太平，此令。

（蒙藏院档案。）

After the Thirteenth Dalai Lama went to India in 1910, the Qing government removed his title. The Grand President of the Republic of China decreed the restoration of the title on October 18, 1912. The decree reads: "Now the Republic of China has been established, and the five nationalities have become a big family. The former Dalai Lama has loyally pledged his allegiance to the central government. The former misunderstanding has disappeared. So the title of *The Loyal, Submissive, Great, Good, Self-Existent Buddha of Heaven* should be restored to the Dalai Lama. It is hoped that he will maintain the Yellow-Hat Faith, support the Republic and enjoy peace together with us."

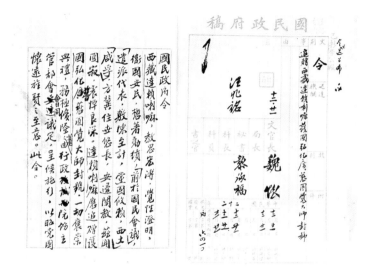

The title of "Great Master of Patriotism, Magnanimity, Benevolence and Sagacity" granted posthumously to the 13th Dalai Lama of Tibet by the Nationalist Government in December 1933.

Tibetan delegates attending China's National Congress and being elected as members of the National Congress.

The Tibetan local government was represented by its delegates at the National Congresses held in 1931, 1936 and 1946.

The 9th Panchen Erdeni and some prominent figures of Tibet were elected and appointed as officials of the Central Government.

In May 1940, the Tibetan local government cabled the Nationalist Government's Office in Tibet about Khenchung Losang Drashi, Tsedrung Thubten Triley and Thubten Senge being appointed as the Tibetan delegates to the National Congress.

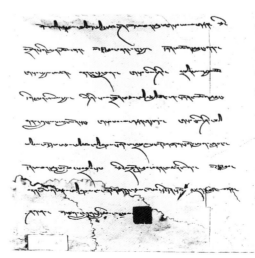

The Nationalist Government issued the following decree: "Lhamo Dondrup shall be enthroned as the Fourteenth Dalai Lama without the confirmation formalities."

Before the enthronement of the 14th Dalai Lama on February 22, 1940, the Nationalist Government sent Wu Zhongxin to Lhasa as special envoy to examine the reincarnation of the 13th Dalai Lama. In the picture is Wu Zhongxin.

On January 26, 1940, the Regent Radreng (Rwa-sgreng) Rimpoche made a formal request through Wu Zhongxin to the Chinese Central Government for the omission of the formalities of "drawing lots from the golden urn" in the confirmation of Lhamo Dondrup as the 14th Dalai Lama (picture 1).

In response to Wu Zhongxin's cable, the Executive Yuan asked, in a formal report dated January 31, the Nationalist Government to issue a decree confirming Lhamo Dondrup as the 14th Dalai Lama and to grant a sum of money to meet the expenses of his enthronement (picture 2).

On May 2, Lin Sen, President of the Nationalist Government, issued a decree consenting to the succession of Lhamo Dondrup as the 14th Dalai Lama and appropriating 400,000 *yuan* to meet the expenses of his enthronement (picture 3).

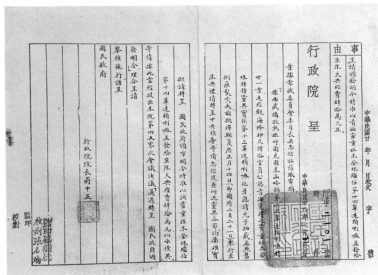

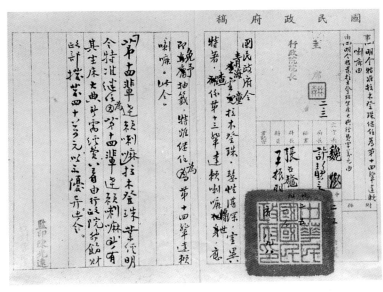

1951

Peaceful Liberation of Tibet

On May 23, 1951, delegates with full powers of the Local Government of Tibet and delegates with full powers of the Central People's Government signed "The Agreement on Measures for the Peaceful Liberation of Tibet." The Fourteenth Dalai Lama and the Tenth Panchen Erdeni cabled the central authorities to express their support of the Agreement.

In September 1954 the Fourteenth Dalai Lama and the Tenth Panchen Erdeni and other Tibetan representatives attended the First Session of the First National People's Congress. The Fourteenth Dalai Lama was elected as Vice-Chairman of the Standing Committee, and the Tenth Panchen Erdeni was elected as member of the Standing Committee of the National People's Congress.

In April 1956 the Preparatory Committee for the Tibet Autonomous Region was founded; the Fourteenth Dalai Lama and the Tenth Panchen Erdeni were elected as the chairman and vice-chairman of the Preparatory Committee respectively.

The Agreement of the Central People's Government and the Local Government of Tibet on Measures for the peaceful Liberation of Tibet (Tibetan text).

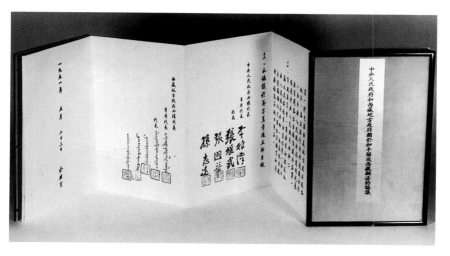

The Agreement of the Central People's Government and the Local Government of Tibet on Measures for the Peaceful Liberation of Tibet (Chinese text).

The Agreement of the Central People's Government and the Local Government of Tibet on Measures for the Peaceful Liberation of Tibet (Abridged)

1. The Tibetan people shall unite and drive out imperialist aggressive forces from Tibet; the Tibetan people shall return to the family of the motherland—the People's Republic of China.

3. In accordance with the policy towards nationalities laid down in the Common Program of the Chinese People's Political Consultative Conference, the Tibetan people have the right exercise national regional autonomy under the unified leadership of the Central People's Government.

4. The central authorities will not alter the existing political system in Tibet. The central authorities also will not alter the established status, functions and powers of the Dalai Lama. Officials of various ranks shall hold offices as usual.

5. The estbblished status, functions and powers of the Panchen Erdeni shall be maintained.

11. In matters related to various reforms in Tibet, there will be no compulsion on the part of the central authorities. The local government of Tibet should carry out reforms of its own accord, and demands for reform raised by the people shall be settled by means' of consultation with the leading personnel of Tibet.

The Agreement of the Central People's Government and the Local Government of Tibet on Measures for the Peaceful Liberation of Tibet stipulates:

"The Tibetan people shall unite and drive out imperialist aggressive forces from Tibet; the Tibetan people shall return to the family of the motherland—the People's Republic of China." In accordance with the policy towards nationalities laid down in the Common Program of the Chinese People's Political Consultative Conference, the Tibetan people have the right to exercise national regional autonomy under the unified leadership of the Central People's Government.

On May 23, 1951, the Agreement on Measures for the Peaceful Liberation of Tibet was signed in Beijing by the delegates of the Tibet Local Government —Ngapo Ngawang Jigme, Khemey Sonam Wangdu, Thubten Tenthar, Thubten Lekmon and Samposey Tenzin Thundup—and the delegates of the Central People's Government —Li Weihan, Zhang Jingwu, Zhang Guohua and Sun Zhiyuan. Vice-chairman Zhu De, Vice-chairman Li Jishen, and Vice-premier Chen Yun attended the ceremony.

45

主席閲

等級 ᴀᴀᴀᴀ   台來   A   No. 55

軍聯A No. 176   收情   類

附註 抄 ABCDF、陳雲、蕭、統戰、民委

中央：

茲將達賴喇嘛給毛主席的兩份電報譯轉如下：

(甲) 中央人民政府毛主席：

今年西藏地方政府特派全權代表噶倫阿沛等五人於

一九五一年四月底抵達北京，與中央人民政府指定的全

權代表進行和談。雙方代表在友好基礎上已于一九五一

年五月二十三日簽訂了關於和平解放西藏辦法的協議。

西藏地方政府及藏族僧俗人民一致擁護，拜在毛主席及

中央人民政府領導下積極協助人民解放軍進藏部隊鞏固

國防，驅逐帝國主義勢力出西藏，保護祖國領土主權的

統一，謹電奉聞。

The 14th Dalai Lama cabled to Chairman Mao Zedong on October 24, 1951: "...The Tibetan local government as well as the ecclesiastical and secular people support the Agreement on Measures for the Peaceful Liberation of Tibet and will, under the leadership of Chairman Mao and the Central People's Government, actively support the People's Liberation Army in Tibet to consolidate national defense, drive out imperialist influences from Tibet and safeguard the unification of the territory and the sovereignty of the motherland. I hereby cable you to inform you of this."

新 成 B / 2 號　　　　　　　　　A 成 No. 1　毛澤東 十一月 日

1949. 11.

附註 已抄 A B C D E F 岳木 總編室 陳實鄰

內容　西藏班禪上書毛主席、朱總司令

總社：

西藏班禪額爾德尼，於十一月一日呈毛主席朱總司令及彭副總司令兩封信，照轉上前決定。

上毛主席朱總司令電：

青海省人民軍政委員會主任事呈北京中央人民政府主席毛中國人民解放軍總司令朱鈞鑒鈞座

以大智大勇之略，成救國救民之業。義師所至，全國騰歡。班禪世受國恩，備荷優崇，廿餘年來，為了西藏領土主權之完整，呼籲奔走未嘗稍懈，第以未獲結果良用疚心。刻下羈留青海待命返藏。茲幸任

鈞座領導之下，西北已獲解放，中央人民政府成立，凡有血氣，同聲鼓舞。今後人民之康樂可期，國家之復興有望，西藏解放指日可待。班禪謹代表全藏人民向鈞座致崇高無上之敬意，並矢誠擁護愛戴之忱。班禪額爾德尼叩十月一日

印

In a telegraphic message to Chairman Mao Zedong and Commander-in-Chief Zhu De on October 1, 1949, from Qinghai, the Panchen Erdeni said: "... These accomplishments will surely bring peace and happiness to the people and make it possible for the nation to stand on its feet again; and with these accomplishments the liberation of Tibet is only a matter of time..."

47

The Wheel of Dharma presented by the Fourteenth Dalai Lama to Chairman Mao in 1954 with an inscription in the Tibetan and Chinese languages, which can be summarized as follows: When attending the First National People's Congress as a Tibetan delegate in 1954, I, the Dalai Lama, offered respectfully, according to the Tibetan politico-religious convention, this golden Wheel of Dharma to Chairman Mao, great leader of all nationalities of China, to express our best wishes.

The present offered by the Tenth Panchen Erdeni to Chairman Mao.

Both the Fourteenth Dalai Lama and the Tenth Panchen Erdeni attended the First Session of the First National People's Congress.

The picture shows the Dalai Lama and the Panchen Erdeni casting their votes on the adoption of China's first constitution.

PART TWO

THE FEUDAL SERF SYSTEM IN TIBET BEFORE 1959

A Society Based on a Regime that Combined the Political and Religious Powers, and Divided People into Three Strata and Nine Grades

Tibet before 1959 had a society of feudal serfdom. Along with the general characteristics of feudal serfdom, there were many remnants of slavery. This social system was more cruel and reactionary than serfdom in Europe in the Middle Ages. The serf-owners' economic interests were protected by a political system that combined political and religious powers, ruling over the Tibetan people spiritually as well as politically. The local government of Tibet (in Tibetan, *Kashag*, meaning "the institute that issues orders") was composed of powerful and influential monks and aristocrats. It upheld a series of social, political and legal institutions that rigidly stratified society. *The Thirteen Laws* and *The sixteen Laws* divided the Tibetan people into three strata in nine grades according to their family background and social status.

The Organization of the Tibetan Regime

The *Kashag* headed by the Dalai Lama was an organ of political authority of the joint dictatorship over the region exercised by Tibetan aristocrats and monks. It was composed of four *kalons* —three laymen and one monk. Below the *Kashag*, the most important administrative organs, were the *Yigtsang* and *Tsekhang*. The *Yigtsang*, consisting of four chief secretaries, all monks, was responsible for drawing up various documents, taking care of the seal of the Dalai Lama, planning the appointment and removal of local officials and coordinating the relations between the monasteries and the local government. The Tsekhang, composed of four lay officials, handled affairs concerning local finance, the issuing of decrees and the training of lay officials.

Under the *Kashag* government were the prefectures and *dzongs* (counties).

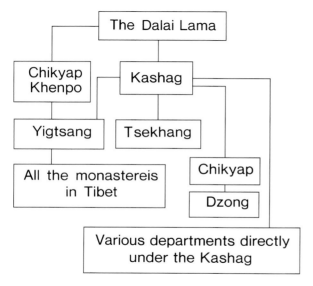

Rigidly Stratified Tibetan Society

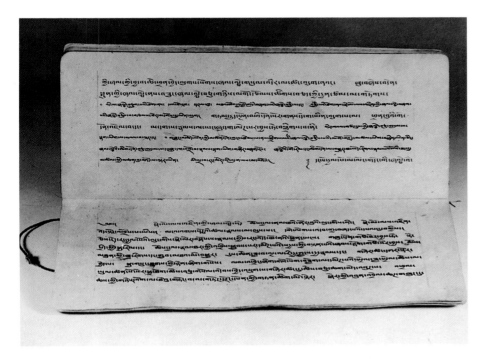

In 1613. Karma Tenkyong Wangpo ordered *The Thirteen Laws* to be compiled by deleting two articles out of the ancient *Fifteen Articles of Law*. *The Thirteen Laws* continued to be used until 1959.

The Sixteen Laws were a Tibetan feudal legal code compiled by Pesewa by order of Karma Tenkyong Wangpo in the early seventeenth century. They were based on *The Fifteen Laws*, with some additions and deletions, making them more concrete. Compared with *The Fifteen Laws*, the *Sixteen Laws* have an additional article, Article 16, "Law for the non-Tibetan areas." After the *Kashag* government was established, *The Sixteen Laws* had continued to be used until 1959.

Article 7 of *The Thirteen Laws* "A law on the price of life" (abstract)

The old law said: "When King Yashe (Yar-tshe) was killed by the Hor (Hor-rgyal-po), the compensation for his life was his body's weight of gold. King Gesar was killed by the Dengkes, his life was so precious that the Dengkes could not offer the compensation."

People were divided into three strata: upper, middle and lower. The life price for those belonging to the top grade of upper stratum is very high. They could not be killed except in wars. If anyone of them was murdered, the compensation was claimed for his life in land and alluvial gold instead of cash and valuables. As to those from the middle grade of upper stratum down through to the lower grade of lower stratum, the price of their lives was fixed and compensation paid in cash or valuables.

People were divided into three strata according to their blood, social position, and profession. In most cases the division was decided in accordance with social position and power. Official position, or lack of it, was also taken into consideration.

According to the old law, the life-price of a blacksmith or a butcher and their kind was a straw rope. Women, tramps, beggars, black-smiths and butchers were in the lower grade of the lower stratum.

The Social Strata Stipulated in Tibetan Local Codes

Upper Stratum:

Upper grade: the King of Tsang and other highest rulers of Tibet (whose life-price was priceless);

Middle grade: Geshes, teachers of morals, abbots, and highranking officials;
[headmen who had more than 300 attendants and servants, *dzongpons*, and *khenpos*, (whose lifeprice was 300-400 taels of silver)];

Lower grade: middle-rank officials, monks;
[lamas of *dratsang* (Buddhist colleges), *bikchu* (full-ordained monks), and government officials on the *drungkhor* level who had 300 attendants and servants (whose life-price was 200 taels of silver)]

Middle stratum:

Upper grade: common officials, *senpons* (in charge of the Dalai's bed chamber), and office worker under officials;
knights under *drungkhor*, administrators and supervisors of *dratsang* (whose life-price was 140-150 taels of silver)

Middle grade: Middle-rank clerks;
[*dzapa* of minor monasteries (whose life-price was 50-70 taels of silver)]

Lower grade: commoners;
[lay aristocrats (whose life-price was 30-40 taels of silver)]

Lower stratum:

Upper grade: [independent bachelors, servants doing odd-jobs in government offices (whose life-price was 30 taels of silver)]

Middle grade: [blacksmiths, butchers, and beggars who had permanent residence and paid taxes (whose life-price was 20 taels of silver)]

Lower grade: [Women, beggars, butchers, and blacksmiths (whose life-price was a straw rope)]

Note: This table is compiled according to *The Thirteen Laws* and *The Sixteen Laws*. Phrases within the square brackets [   ] are quoted from *The Sixteen Laws*.

The Structure of Tibetan Society

Ratio of Population Between the Feudal Manorial Lords and Their Serfs in 1959

Total Tibetan population	980,000
Feudal manorial lords	5%
Serfs	95%

The manorial lords of Tibet comprised the officials of the former Tibetan local government, the aristocrats and monasteries (upper-strata lamas) and their agents.

There were 400 noble families in Tibet. By 1959, members from 197 noble families worked in the Kashag. Among these families 25 were big noble families, 26 middle noble families and 146 petty noble families.

Serf-owners lived a luxurious, decadent life. Pictured here is the bed-room of Trijang Lozang Yeshe, a serf-owner.

The serfs were members of the "thralpa" and "dudchong" strata.

The *thralpas*, who accounted for 60-70 percent of the serfs, were persons doing unpaid labor for the serf-owners. The picture shows *thralpas* carrying goods to the Potala.

Nangzan, a Tibetan word meaning "fed in the house," were slaves.

Five percent of the Tibetans were house slaves, called *Nangzan*. Without means of production or personal freedom, they were considered by serf-owners as "livestock that can speak." Pictured here is Tsering Drolma, a *Nangzan*, who lived under the lavatory of the lord.

Dudchong, meaning small household, were made up of bankrupt *thraplas*. Their social status was still lower than that of *thralpas*, and they lived a still poorer life than the *thralpas* did. They accounted for 30-40 percent of serfs. Pictured here is the Nganan family living in the manger of the manorial lord.

The Feudal Lords' Ownership of Means of Production

The monasteries, officialdom and the aristocrats owned all the arable land and pastures as well as overwhelming majority of livestock. These means of production were granted to them by the Dalai Lama. They had the right to govern and inherit the land.

Certificate of the Fourteenth Dalai Lama granting Tatra (Stag- brag) the perpetual ownership of the serfs and cattle and sheep of twenty tribes in the Zangzhung area and exempting them from all corvée.

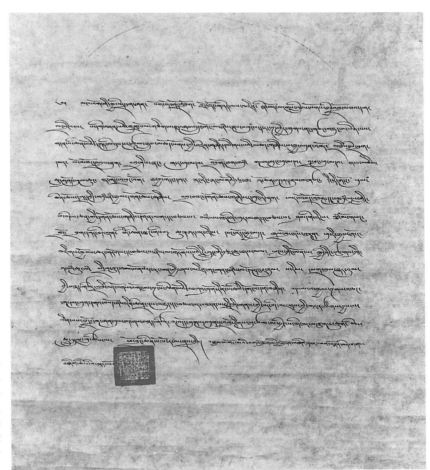

Proclamation issued by the Tibetan Local Government decreeing that the Sakya Monastery's land, manors, pastures and taxes should be protected from encroachment and the monastery be exempted from corvée service.

The Sakyapa and Gelugpa are identical in their religious doctrine and system. Our forefathers have always been concerned for us. No one on horseback sent on errands by post staging station or military camps is allowed to cause damage to the manors of Sakya Monastery. The manors provide support to the monastery in its religious ceremonies, food and tea, monastic study and sacrificial offerings. The manors include Tripai-Drama, Langthong-Dranbu, Drashigang, three pastures at the pass of Khala valley, the land in Yarlung and Chang valley near Sakya, the pastures of Phichun in the lower reaches of the Kyichu River, Trago, Dongkar, Gangring-Ganggo to the south of Lhasa, three manors of Gyantse Monastery in the east and west of Mt. Kachog, Tingri and Chugasi, the Ralung-Ribu manor of Dranzang Monastery, the manors and branch-monasteries of Debalingkha (bde-bagling-kha) Monastery in the pastoral areas of North Tibet and Pusong, the mountain village of Samyalanesu (bsam-Yas-la sne-su), Shabgeding, Drimayong, Drikar-Dedan, Palchen-Changsa, Chukha-Phagdan, Wangdul-Gyadul, Shedrag-Todan, and Mt. Sharngo-gichog.

It is also forbidden to do any damage to the grass, trees, forests, (natural and planted) ditches and rivers. By order of the Fifth Dalai Lama, this certificate is issued to grant the Oracle Ngawang Kunga Sonam Rinchen and his descendants the authority which will last as long as Buddhism exists. All people, high or low, should behave discreetly, neither making trouble nor encroaching on the Monastery's property.

The Potala (seal)
On auspicious day of
Water-Serpent year.

Comment: The former Dalai Lamas' instruction have been carried out smoothly up to the present. They should be carried out in the future as they had always been.

Certificate issued by the Sixth Dalai Lama, granting land to the Zhalu Monastery

The All-Knowing Great Master Buton was Buddhist sun shining in the Tibetan region. Tsongkhapa learnt the Buddhist sutras of Vajrayana from his disciples. The 5th Dalai Lama studied the sutras and took vows from Sonam Chosdrub, abbot of the Zhalu Monastery. I also studied Buddhism from Yonten Jungnas, abbot of the Zhalu Monastery, so the monastery should be protected. All the property of the Zhalu Monastery and Ribu Monastery, for example, their manors in Kanad, Drucho, etc., and all their land and servants including bricklayers shall be protected without exception.

If disputes occur and worsen between manors, they must be settled promptly by the abbot and other administrators of the Zhalu Monastery.

This is a supplement to the deed granted by the Fifth Dalai Lama to the Zhalu Monastery.

Issued in the jia-chen *year of Kangxi reign.*

The Seventh Dalai Lama reaffirmed that the King of Lhagyari should enjoy forever all the rights granted to him through old and new documents.

Lhagyariwa's family have followed the faith of the Gelugpa sect of Tsongkhapa for many generations. Ever since the Second Dalai Lama, the Lhagyariwas have been benefactors of the religion and respected all the Dalai Lama... When I was born in Kham, he sent Lozang Konchog to offer presents to me. For such piety he should be protected. All the dzongs, Shikas, land, and serfs that originally belonged to him will be owned by him according to the stipulations issued prior to the year of Rabbit. When Tagtse was in power, some households of Lhagyariwa surrendered. After mediation, it was decided that Lhagyariwa should pay taxes for Lukhang who had surrendered... The taxes of Chungpa and those whose names have not yet registered should be delivered to Lhangyariwa.

Issued in the tenth month of the Iron-Sheep year at the Potala.

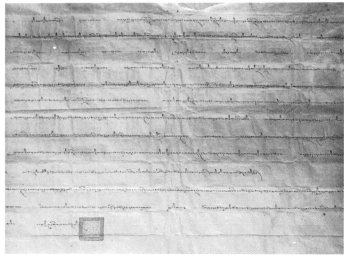

The Fourteenth Dalai Lama's proclamation that the Living Buddha Thubten Nyingdra's successor should have the right to inherit the manors and pastures of his monastery.

Proclamation issued by the Dalai Lama bestowing large tracts of land to manors such as Tripal Drama and Yalung Dragang, and the serfs on the land upon the Sakya Monastery to be its property.

The Sakya family are divinely descended. They propagate Buddhism and do good for the people, so they should be protected. Particularly, the Sakyapa and Gelugpa sects are related in origin. Certificates have been given to the Sakyas Monastery about its ownership of land and serfs... As the Sakya Monastery benefits Buddhist believers, its manors such as Tripal Drama, Yarlung Dragang, etc., and all the fiefs granted to it ever since Kunga Lodro will never be taken from it.

Issued on the third day of the twelfth month in the Wood-Hog year at the Potala.

**The three major catego-
ries of feudal lords, who accounted for about five percent of the Tibetan population, controlled 95 percent of
the material base on which
the masses of serfs relied for
existence.**

---

*Arable Land Owned by the Three Catego-
ries of Feudal Lords in 1959:*
Total amount of arable land in Tibet:
3,300,000 *khal* (a *khal* is equivalent to a
Chinese *mu*, or 1/15 of a hectare).
The local government officials owned
1,283,700 *khal*, making up 38.9%.
Aristocrats owned 790,000 *Khal*, making
up 24%.
The high clergy owned 1,214,400 *khal*,
making up 36.8%.

The feudal lords owned total grassland and
the overwhelming majority of livestock. For
instance, in Ngamring County of Shigatse
Prefecture the feudal lords owned 70% of
livestock, and the common people owned
30% of livestock.

The Feudal Lords' Ownership of Their Serfs

Serfs and slaves accounted for 95 percent of the Tibetan population (peasants 60%, herdsmen 20%, lower-class monks 15%). They were owned by serf-owners, just like the means of production. They had no political rights or personal freedom. They and their children were freely given away as gifts or donations, sold or exchanged for goods. Their marriages had to be approved in advance by their manorial lords. Serfs who married out of the mano-rial estate had to pay ransom money to their lords. Those who could not perform corvée or went out to seek a livelihood elsewhere should pay "corvée taxes" to show their dependence on the lords. If a serf lost his ability to work, his *thralkang* field, livestock and farm tools would be confiscated by the lord. The property of those who died without issue was confiscated.

A serf's child was born to be a serf of its parent's lord. The picture shows a serf bringing her newborn child for registration at her manorial lord's house and for payment of poll-tax.

Manorial lords could exchange their serfs. This is a certificate for the exchange of serfs between the Richo Monastery and Pongyashung.

Translation of a contract

Ngodrup, son of the door-keeper and serf of the Richo monastery, is now exchanged with Tenzin Wangyal, son of Drakar and Jamyang Wangyal, who are serfs of Pongyashung, by the decision of the monastery and its patron. In the future, Ngodrup's descendants will all belong to the lord Pongyashung, while Tenzin Wangyal's descendants will belong to the Richo monastery.

The contract is concluded to ensure that there will be no disputes between the two parties on this subject. There are two copies of this contract, which will serve as certification.

Treasurer Shengri (seal affixed)
Kyiso of Richo (official seal affixed)
on the first day of the sixth month
of Water-Tiger year by the
Tibetan calendar

Manorial lords could make presents of their serfs to others. This is a certificate by which a monastery's "Lharang" gave its serfs Tsering Dorje, Kunzang (female), and Song Butri (female) and their future descendants to be servants in the Drawo Official Residence.

The following statement has been confirmed by the Lharang in the Earth-Sheep year, never to be changed.

A certificate was issued in the Wood-Rat year to the effect that the Lharang granted land and serfs to two high lamas of the Drawo Residence. As the two lamas left for deep meditation in seclusion, the Dratsang took back the serfs. Now for lack of servants, Palwang, the steward of the Residence, has asked the Dratsang to send Tsering Dorje, Kunzang (female), and Song Butri (female) to Residence as servants. In the future, the application of this kind of thing will be made by the monks of the Dratsang.

Manorial lords could transfer their serfs to others at will .This is a contract by which the Nechung Monastery gave its serf to Tshalpa Drongdopa, for compensation.

Translation of A Contract

Lhapa, daughter of Sonam Butri, who is the serf of Nechung Dratsang, was brought up by Edingpa. The chief steward of the abbot of the Nechung monastery has paid Edingpa twelve tsamka for his care for Lhapa.

Now Lhapa is transferred to Tshalpa Drongdopa. It is deci ded that Tshalpa Drongdopa should perform unconditionally all kinds of corvée and work assigned to him by Buddhist officials. The girl, Lhapa, should also do her best to offer service.

In the future, the girl's marriage may be decided by Tshalpa Drongdopa or by herself, but her descendants should be on the list of ula laborers of the Nechung monastery. This stipulation must be observed. Violators will be severely punished.

Contractor: Drongdopa
Lhapa (finger-print)
Guarantor: Gyalbu (finger-print)
on the tenth day of the second month of Fire-Dragon year by Tibetan calendar.

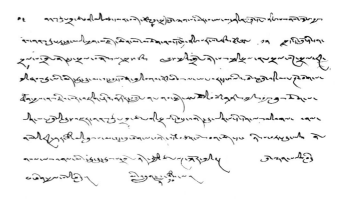

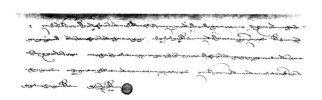

Serfs were forced to perform various covrée duties. Reproduced here is an official decision that serf Zhiwa Metog should work as a servant-nun in the Drakar Nunnery of the Richo Monastery.

Zhiwa Metog, daughter of Birika Chonkhangpa, was sent to be a nun at the Drakar nunnery. Zhiwa Metog had married Tsering Paldron, a serf of the nunnery, before she entered the nunnery. Tsering Paldron was ordered to serve the nuns, but he had no daughter. Therefore, Zhiwa Metog and her child were sent to do corvée labor in the nunnery. Be it noted that Zhiwa Metog is no longer a member of the Birika Chonkhangpa family.

The twenty-seventh day of the eighth month in Water-Monkey year.

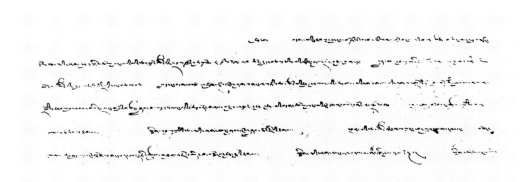

Serfs had to pay off debts by doing corvée. This certificate records that Drashi Choda instructed his sister Tsering Lhamo to pay off his debts by doing covrée labor for the monastery "Lharang" for ten years.

Translation of a Contract

I, the undersigned, confirm that the following contract has been concluded of my own free will and is never to be changed.

I, Drashi Choda belong to the Nari Monastery of the Nari Manor. I borrowed 34 khal and 3 sheng of grain from the Lharang granary in the Wood-Monkey year, the interest of which amount to 6 khal and 14.5 sheng. The principal and the interest total 40 khal and 19.3 sheng of grain. As I am unable to pay back the sum annually, I ask my younger sister Tsering Lhamo, who shares weal and woe with me, to pay off my debts by doing ten years' unpaid service for the Lharang beginning at the first day of the twelfth month of this Fire-Dog year.

Centificate of the sale of Tsering, a serf in Nagchu.

A contract by which the Namgyal Dratsang exchanged serfs with Gyu-me (the Lower Tantric College).

The Serfs' Economic Burden

Taxes and levies in Tibetan areas included land rent, stock rent, corvée and taxes.

The main form of land rent was forced labor. In addition, there was a mixed form of land rent, which was paid in kind, forced labor and cash.

The manorial lords generally kept 70 percent of their land under their own management and rented out the rest to their serfs as *thralkang* land. The serf tenants of the *thralkang* land also had to till the land managed by the manorial lord, using their own farm animals and tools. The entire harvest on land managed by the manorial lords belonged to them alone.

The serfs had to do corvée for manorial lords and local government and pay taxes in kind and cash. Corvée duties were allotted by the local government.

There were two kinds of stock rent: paid in animal products to the manorial lords according to the original number of livestock rented from them, or in products according to the actual number of livestock.

Other taxes included land tax, corvée tax, and countless others.

Convée

During the busy farming season, because able-bodied serfs had to perform corvée for their manorial lords, only old people and children were left to work on their "contracted fields."

In payment of land rent, all serfs who tilled land rented from their manorial lords had to do farm work on land directly managed by the manorial lords.

Tab. 2: Taxes and Levies a *Thralpa's* (Serf's) Household Had to Offer in a Year

Name: Lhapa Triley
Place: Rongdu Manor, Medrogunkar
Year: 1949

Unpaid labor	Levies in kind	Taxes in money
1. Short-distance courier station service	1. Grain-tribute to the imperial court	1. Money paid for military service
2. Transportation service	2. Grain paid to post office	2. Money paid for the charcoal for the British
3. Service as a groom for the *dzong* (county) government	3. Grain paid for crossing river by boat	3. Money paid for charcoal
4. Transporting butter for the government	4. Gifts offered to post masters	4. Money paid for the newly recruited soldiers
5. Transporting riverdeer fur	5. Rape oil paid to the government	5. *Rgya-bsu* (money offered for receiving officials)
6. Transporting wool	6. Rape oil paid to the Drigung monastery	6. *Skyel-dod* (money offered for seeing off officials)
7. Transporting fur	7. Fodder paid to Drigung monastery	7. Tax paid for rape oil
8. Transporting butter for monasteries	8. Gifts offered to the officials in charge of salt	
9. Transporting wood and charcoal	9. Salary in kind to the headman of Tonggai	
10. Transporting charcoal for the British	10. Grain paid for preventing hailstorms	
11. Transporting rape oil	11. Grain paid for receiving and seeing off officials	
12. Transporting rape oil for the Drigung monastery		
13. Transporting fodder for the Drigung monastery		
14. Transporting charcoal to Lhasa		
15. Odd jobs		
16. Chopping firewood		
17. Repairing houses		
18. Service as a messenger		
19. Long-distance courier station service		

Picture caption:

Serfs were overburdened with scores of kinds of levies collected by the Tibetan local government and *dzong* and *shika*. Heavy physical work accounted for 60-80 percent of their total labor. In addition, there were levies in kind under numerous names, for instance, the levies on medicine, dyestuffs, tiger-skins, and fruits in the Tsona Dzong (county), levies on paper and woolen fabric in Gongkar Dzong (county), levies on meat in the Chonggye Dzong (county), etc. This is a list of levies a Thralpa (serf) of a manor in Medrogunkar Dzong had to pay.

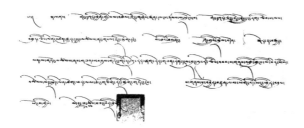

"Traffic Certificate" (A claim on corvée on a journey)

This is an official notice to the headmen and common people of all the dzong and shi along the road from Lhasa to Gongkar:

Sholdron Rabtsepa, the newly-appointed dzongpon of Gongkar, is going to assume his office. The inhabitants along the road he is traveling are responsible for arranging and supplying lodging, firewood, a sheep-skin raft and no more than eight horses for him. Forage will be prepared as soon as horses are sent to him. The forage for each horse per day is converted into five liang of sliver, which must be paid in full. All this sum of money is to be allotted among the local people responsible for the duty. The money is collected for the expenses on a two-way journey. As soon as he arrives, the traffic certificate will be returned.

Issued on the twenty-sixth day of the twelfth month of the Fire-Cock year by Tibetan calendar (stamped with a government seal).

Agreement made by public representatives of four dzongs on presenting a petition to local authorities for reducing corvée (main content):

The expenses for the board and lodging, firewood, wages and other items for the laborers sent by the order of the authorities to construct the Chokorje Monastery and Dargang as well as the official mansion of Lhokyi (the Shannan Governor's mansion) are excessive. The long-term and short-term taxes levied for the constructions are limitless. All this makes people complain of the suffering from the burden, which is too heavy for them. Therefore, the public representatives of the four dzongs agree to make a petition to the authorities. They will meet in Nedong on the fifteenth of the following month and then start their jouney together. The agreement is signed by

Drogya (chief public representative from Jamdon)
Dingrab Sonam Dorje (public representative from Talang)
Woser (public representative from Gyadu)
Akon Drashi (public representative from Lhaso)
on the twenty-fifth day of the twelfth month of the Iron-Dragon year.

The Distribution of Grain in a Manor
(Example: Dalongdra Manor in 1959)

Total area of land: 1,455 *khal*
Grain harvest: 74,088 kg., of which
        64,260 kg. (86.7% of the total) went to the feudal lords.
        9,828 kg. (13.3%) went to his serfs.

When the *Kashag* government issued a *ula* tablet for corvée service, the serfs had to perform all the services required of them by the *ula* tablet (obilgation to serve official travelers). One form of corvée required serfs to carry officials on the back when climbing mountains.

Usury

All the manorial lords in old Tibet practiced usury. They forced their serfs to accept usurious loans. It was very common for the serfs to have loan debts. The rates charged by the manorial lords were so high that many debtors were unable to discharge their debts, and even their children were unable to do it, so the debts became "descendants' debts". Anyone wanting to contract a loan had to get several families to give security for him. If the debtor went bankrupt or fled, the families who went bail for him had to repay the amount owed.

Debts of the serfs of Drepung Monastery in 1959

Number of serfs: 20,000	
Total highland barley owed as debt	10,000,000 *khal* (equivalent to 140,000,000 kg.)
Average per capital debt (in barley)	500 *khal* (equivalent to 7,000 kg.)
Total money debt	13,330,000 silver dollars
Average per capital debt in money	666.5 silver dollars

A contract signed by Tsewang Rabten and his wife to repay debts by giving up their daughter and young son (main content): Being unable to pay back the money and grain they owe Nedong Dekhang, Tsewang Rabten and his wife, serfs of the Dusong Manor, must give up their daughter Gensong Tonten and younger son Padma Tenzin to Dekhang to repay the debts. The descendants of their son and daughter will be Dekhang's serfs.

Contract signed by Drashi Choda for paying back his debt by letting his sister Tsering Lhamo work for Lharang without pay for ten years (main content):

Drashi Chuda, a serf of Nari Manor, is unable to pay off the forty khal (equivalent to about 560 kilograms) of grain he owes Lharang, so he will allow his sister Tsering Lhamo to pay off his debt by doing ten years' unpaid services for Lharang.

The contract stipulates: "In case of violation of the contract, Drashi Chuda shall be punished according to the local law."

The Oppression of the Serfs by Manorial Lords

In Tibet under the serfdom, not only did the local regime at various levels set up judicial institutions, but the big monasteries, manorial lords and tribal chieftains could also judge cases and had their own private prisons.

If the serfs stood up against the manorial lords, violated the law or could not pay rent or taxes in time, the lords would punish them according to the *Thirteen Laws* or other laws. They used such inhuman tortures as gouging out the eyes, cutting off the feet or hands, pushing the condemned person down from cliff, drowning, beheading, etc.

Article 3 of The Thirteen Laws (abstract):

"Those who stir up a row before the king's palace shall be arrested; those who fight with weapon shall be arrested; the beggars who steal shall be arrested; those who loot shall be arrested. Persons of low social status who quarrel with those of high status shall be arrested."

Article 4 of The Thirteen Laws *(abstract):*

"Those who loot, kidnap, steal and kill, murder, or rebel against the authorities shall be punished corporally by: gouging out the eyes, cutting off the foot, tongue or hand, being pushed off a cliff, drowning, or execution. They shall be punished according to the degrees of their crimes."

The eighth article of The Thirteen Laws

"*The law of compensation for blood*" (abstract):

The old law said: "A drop of blood of the people of high status is worth one qian of silver, while a drop of blood of the people of low status is worth one li (one-tenth of a qian) of silver."

There is a difference between the harm done to people of high status and those of low status. If a commoner wounds an official, the commoner shall be punished by cutting off his hand or foot. If a lord wounds his servant accidentally, the lord shall not be punished if the servant had been cured. No compensation shall be given if a lord beats his servant to death.

Serf Bupa's eyes were gouged out by his manorial lord.

A herdsman named Bemo Honzin had his right hand cut off just because he stole a small bag of *qingke* (highland barley) from his manorial lord's house.

Tuto, a herdsman from Amdo, had his foot cut off
by the headman of his tribe.

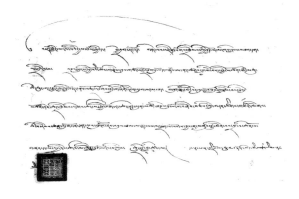

To Dzonapons, *secretaries and all officials:*
All criminal cases, great or small, including murder, occuring in the manors in Ü-Tsang and North Tibet under the jurisdiction of Kyiso (chief of the financial department) of the Drepung Monastery, must be heard and decided by the Kyiso himself. The final decisions including those concerning murder committed by officials, aristocrats of common people shall be decided by the Kyiso according to the severity of the crime. All the fines and confiscated property shall be given to the monastery for its funds. This has become a special traditional institution. No other organizations shall refuse to follow it on the pretext that the fine is too severe. Drepung is quite different from other monasteries. All the fine and confiscated property must be given to it.

All traditional institutions must be observed conscientiously. This notice is issued on the sixth day of the fifth month of the Water-Monkey year.

Part of the instruments used to torture serf-prisoners in the Nangtseshag (police station of Lhasa).

Instruments of torture: leather thonged whips; leather face- slappers

Instruments of torture: finger-presses

Two wooden frame and fetters that the serf Geleg of Tsunpa village of Lhunze county was compelled to wear for twelve years.

Instruments of torture: instrument for gouging out the eyes

Instruments of torture: iron fetters; handcuffs

After cutting off the victim's hand or foot, the executioner plunged the stump into a pot of boiling oil to stop the bleeding. Three serfs died a cruel death beside this oil-pot.

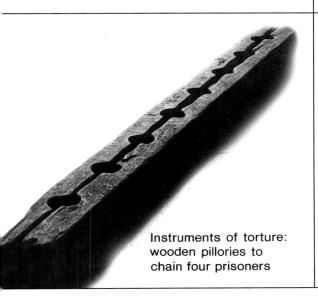

Instruments of torture: wooden pillories to chain four prisoners

Skin of a child

The serf-prisoners were not fed, they have to be beggars on streets.

In 1959, herdsman Bude was telling how his eyes
had been gouged out.

To Rege:
To hold the Buddhist ceremony of sacrifices to the devas, we need four human heads, ten sets of human intestines, pure blood, impure blood, earth from ruins, widow's menstrual blood, leper's blood, various kinds of meat and flesh, human and animal hearts, water the sun has never shone upon, soil raised by a whirlwind, thorns growing facing the north, dog's dung, human excrement, butcher's boots, etc. You are expected to send them to Tsechukang on the twentieth day of the month.

from Tsechukang
on the nineteenth day of the month.

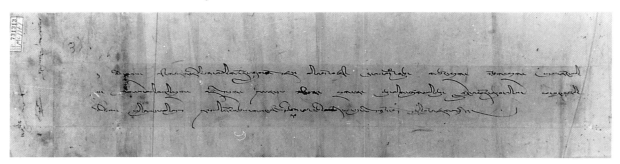

To Headman Redo:
To celebrate the Dalai Lama's birthday, all monks of the Lower Tantric College (Gyu-me Dratsang) should chant the sutras for offering sacrifices to the Overawing Deity. The performance of the Buddhist ritual requires that sacrifices be offered on that day. So you are expected to provide immediately a set of human intestines, two human heads, blood and a whole human skin.

Choskyi Shapekhong

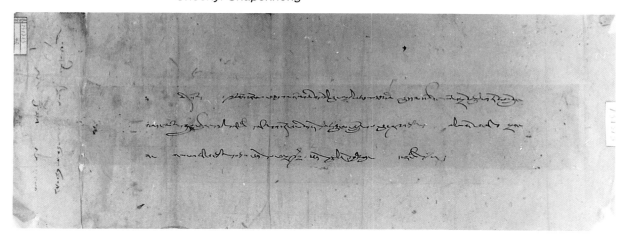

Sangpa, a poor monk, was cruelly maimed.

The Serfs' Miserable life

The wealth of the society was highly concentrated in Tibet before 1959. More than 80 percent was possessed by the manorial lords and less than 20 percent belonged to the serfs, who accounted for 95 percent of the population. The masses of serfs lived in extreme poverty.

Destitute, the herdsman Lhaje wandered far from home and became a beggar.

The hungry and sick child lay by the roadsides.

The hungry children searching foods from garbage on the street.

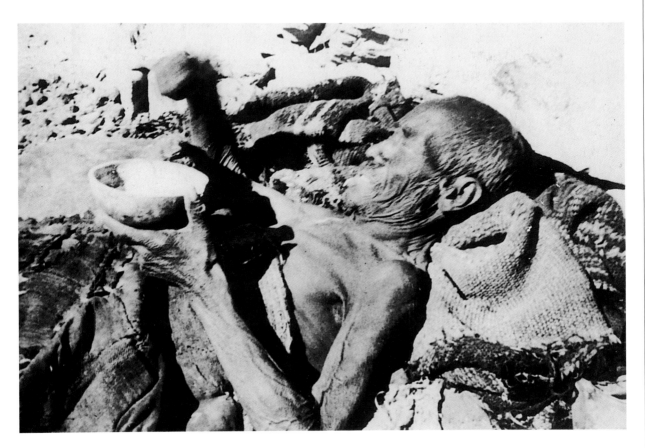

Poverty-stricken, paralyzed old man had to lie on
the street and beg.

The cloth worn for 3 generations
by herdsman Anan's family

The hat worn for 73 years by Chaba Hazhu

Earthen pots and tea utensils used by serfs

The herdsman's farm tools: a plow and hoe

A corner of slum in Lhasa

Some statistics about serfdom in Tibet

Many statistics and data show that in Tibet before 1959, production stagnated, the population of the Tibetan nationality diminished, epidemic diseases prevailed, the people lived in misery and society as a whole developed very slowly. The facts cited above give a broad outline.

Population of Tibet

1737 (the second year of the Qianlong reign in the Qing dynasty):	1,000,000
1953:	about 1,000,000

Because a lot of serfs had fled, many villages and fields were deserted.

Low Yields of Grain in 1959

For each 14 kg. seeds only 42-70 kg. could be harvested.

Low Breeding Rate of Livestock in 1959 (taking Nagchu as an example)

Cattle: Survival rate
of young cattle   40-50%

        Pregnancy rate   40-50%

Sheep: Survival rate
of lambs   30-50%

        Pregnancy rate   70-80%

Statistics Compiled in an Investigation of Illiteracy in Five Manors in 1949

Total number of adults:	581
Illiterates:	550 (94% of the total)
Literate or beginning to learn:	31 (6%)

Deaths from Epidemic Diseases (1925-1937) in Lhasa Suburbs:

Over 7,000 deaths from smallpox in 1925

Over 2,800 deaths from typhoid fever in 1934

Over 2,000 deaths from typhoid fever in 1937

Statistics of the Runaway Households in Four Village of the Bomi District (1927-1952)

Name of village	Total households in 1927	Total households in 1952	Number of runaway households	Runaway rate %
Sangna	130	3	127	97.6
Denaka	18	8	10	55
Dashin	50	20	30	60
Genang	23	13	10	43
total	221	44	177	80

CONCLUSION

Over a long period of historical development, the Tibetan nationality has created a brilliant culture and made outstanding contributions to the formation and development of China as a multinational unified country.

The feudal serf system of Tibet seriously hindered the progressive development of the Tibetan society. In 1959 under the leadership of the Communist Party of China, through the efforts of the Tibetan people serfdom was abolished and Tibet embarked on the socialist road. Over the past thirty and more years, Tibet has seen drastic changes. Population and production have grown, society has become stable, living standards have been rapidly raised, and education and science and technology are prospering.

ACKNOWLEDGMENT

Sincere acknowledgment is made to all the scholars and professors who have contributed advice and suggestions. Thanks are particularly due to the National Archives Bureau, the Central Archives, No.2 National Archives in Nanjing, the Chinese Centre for Tibetology Studies, Xinhua News Agency, as well as the Translation Centre of Minority Languages and the Central University for Nationalities, for generous permission to make use of their materials and cordial help.